CONTROLLING

ANXIETY

— · —

Use These 13 Techniques and Discover How to Improve Communication in Your Relationships

Rebecca Golden

Rebecca Golden

CONTENTS

INTRODUCTION

D oes fear dominate your thoughts, your actions, and your behavior?

Is it a baseless yet persistent fear that sometimes becomes an endless worry that influences many decisions you make? Do you constantly agonize about getting over the worry and fear that it makes you anxious and riddled with doubt about your mental health that you feel as though you are no longer in control?

What I just described is anxiety on a level that is beyond ordinary.

We all feel anxious and worried at various points in our lives, but it is temporary and disappears once the problems are solved. However, clinical worry and anxiety are often baseless, holding the person dealing with the syndrome in a grip so tight that they long for freedom.

I can offer you that freedom by teaching you a few simple techniques to overcome your anxiety issues. You can learn to be free of constant worry, stress, and anxiety and work on rebuilding your life; learn to form stronger relationships with people, learn to trust more, and be less paranoid.

If you are dealing with high-functioning anxiety, you are probably living an outwardly successful life while dealing with endless turmoil internally. You could be a mom expertly juggling your many roles without hinting at the inner turmoil you are attempting to handle. You may be a professional carrying out an essential job in society, a nurse, a teacher, a CEO, a wife living with a loving husband, or a single woman who seems successful and happy. But unknown to society, you could share similar troubles, worries, and stresses with anxiety as a root cause.

Reaching out for my book is a sign that you recognize the need for help because anxiety is a syndrome that is 100% curable. Still, sadly many people decide to bear the burden until it becomes a more severe and clinical form of depression that is harder to treat.

Let's review a few statistics.

- Generalized anxiety disorder (GAD)—3.1% of the U.S. population is dealing with GAD; however, only 43.2% are seeking help for the disorder, a sad fact because GAD is fully curable.

- Panic Disorder (PD)—Women are more susceptible to PD and have double the chance of acquiring the disorder, which affects a total of 2.7% of the population in the U.S.

- Post-traumatic stress disorder (PTSD)—women are the most susceptible to PTSD. They are five times more sensitive than men when developing PTSD, which affects 3.6% of the U.S. population (Anxiety and Depression Association of America, 2021).

These are only a few surface-level mental health disorders prevalent in our society today. And if you look at how mental health disorders affect the genders, women are more prone to dealing with stress and anxiety.

The age range in which people deal with mental health problems is even more distressing.

- Six percent of children aged 6—11 will harbor some anxiety disorder.

- Ten percent of teens between 12 and 17 will deal with mental health problems.

- Twenty-one percent of adults in the U.S. harbor symptoms of mental health disorders.

- Shockingly, 30- to 44-year-olds are diagnosed the most, with 23% from this age group having mental health problems.

Why Is Anxiety So Prevalent?

Everyone may experience anxiety at one time or another. Still, it is the depth of that anxiety and the justifiable reason behind it that defines anxiety as a general reaction or a mental disorder.

Normal anxiety, a natural reaction to the stress you are feeling, lasts for a short time and then subsides. Anxiety that endures even after the event causing you stress has subsided, or crops up for no reason, is an indication of a generalized anxiety disorder.

Someone with clinical anxiety often deals with internal battles and constant fear that something will go wrong, even though there is no real cause for those fears. Their fears are due to many factors: uncertainty, losing control, being embarrassed, having self-doubt, and low self-esteem, among many other factors.

Such people become their worst enemies, often belittle themselves, and doubt their self-worth. Their worry is so constant that they are emotionally and physically drained.

How Does one Develop an Anxiety Disorder, and Why Is it so Prevalent in Our Society?

Sadly, our modern lifestyles are partially to blame, where expectations are very high, and support is minimal. Stress and anxiety disorders do not suddenly appear; they result from dealing with long-term uncomfortable situations.

It may be a disgruntled husband who puts too much pressure and expectations on his wife. A boss who overworks you mentally and physically, juggling family life with responsibilities as a wife, mother, and daughter, and playing different roles are some examples that lead to anxiety disorders so prevalent in our society.

My experience with anxiety disorders has given me valuable insights into how the syndrome works, its damage, and how much effort it takes to seek help and accept the fact that you suffer from a mental health disorder.

I have watched family and friends struggle to cope in silence with their syndromes while dealing with medication and endless visits to doctors. Worry and stress they are already dealing with while not knowing how to reach out and talk about the battle they are constantly fighting.

As a result of my experiences and watching and learning, I understand how anxiety works and its root causes. I have formulated several natural techniques to calm you and help you overcome your anxiety disorder by opening up to those who care about your well-being and forming stronger bonds and loving relationships.

Included in the last chapter as a bonus is "My Anxiety Journal Workbook." Use it to log your progress and ensure you successfully follow the techniques I will teach you. Make ample use of the therapeutic effects journaling has on anxiety and continue the habit of keeping your anxiety in check.

Each technique discussed here will help you to identify, stop overthinking, become aware of your triggers, stop your anxious thoughts, and heal. I will introduce techniques to aid you on your journey of self-healing by introducing you to the fantastic effects of breathing exercises for calming your mind and stopping panic attacks and anxiety from taking over. Physical activities that help deal with anxious thoughts and stresses and the healing benefits of spiritual connections are included. I will teach you to break free and live your life as you envision.

Chapter 1

— · —

The Beast Known as "Anxiety"

I know it might be hard to understand my anxiety, but I hope today I have given you some clarity. —Tiffaney L Ganci-Breathe (Ganci, 2018)

Let's start by learning more about anxiety disorders. The fear of the unknown is far greater than dealing with an enemy you know. So, let's take away the uncertainty and fear with it.

There are many types of anxiety disorders, and they can include phobias too. You will learn that each type stems from different reasons, external and internal influences. Sometimes the symptoms are open; other times, they can be hidden, so no one knows until the condition progresses too far. You will avoid all that and choose to walk away from the burden you bear.

You are not alone: The Story of Emma Stone and Her Battle with Anxiety.

Award-winning actress Emma Stone admitted to her anxiety and panic attacks evolving when she was just a child. Her first red flag about her condition came as a shock when she suddenly started to panic, thinking her friend's house was on fire while she was there. Emma, then a child, was convinced the house was on fire and was deeply disturbed by her thoughts that kept telling her she was going to die. Of course, the house was not on fire but what

Emma conceived in her mind was a classic symptom of a panic attack where your worry is unreasonable. Still, you have no control over the sudden terror that takes over your mental and physical reactions.

Emma battled anxiety into adulthood until she learned to use anxiety rather than be a victim. Her acting, she says, is successful because she channels her experiences with panic attacks into the roles she plays, thus managing to portray very realistic characters. Are you ready to take control of your anxiety? Start by identifying your condition.

What Is Anxiety Disorder?

The most common mental disorders, anxiety disorders, are centered around intense fear, excessive worry, and dread of uncertainty which can involve exposure to new and different events and situations.

Anxiety, you will be surprised to learn, is a natural reaction that has been prevalent since the time of our stone-age ancestors. Anxiety and worry kept them alert and, therefore, alive. The constant nervousness you sometimes see in animals keeps them from relaxing and forgetting about the dangers lurking nearby. That same theory worked for our ancestors and kept them alert to approaching threats.

However, anxiety disorders have passed the automatic response to protect and alert; they have become a burden in society, a nagging worry that never ends. Women are more challenged than men when dealing with anxiety as a mental health disorder.

Anxiety often leads to avoidance behavior, while fear instigates the fight-or-flight reaction in people. Having over-the-top symptoms of both anxiety and fear will result in a person being diagnosed as dealing with anxiety.

I use the phrase "over-the-top" because clinical anxiety feels uncontrollable. It is felt in excess and is persistent, where you deal with constant feelings of dread and panic long after the event that triggered your anxiety episode has died down. The symptoms may have been present since childhood if you are dealing with anxiety. However, it is not uncommon for adolescents and adults to develop a form of anxiety based on their circumstances. And because mental health conditions can develop due to various reasons or conditions, they are categorized into different types based on the symptoms displayed.

If you feel you could be dealing with a form of anxiety but have not been diagnosed, see how many of the following symptoms you recognize.

- Having a constant feeling of doom as though something terrible is going to happen.

- You tend to sweat excessively, especially when you feel nervous or know you will have to face an uncomfortable situation.

- You get the shakes, or your body starts to tremble as panic takes over, and you may experience an accelerated heartbeat at the same time.

- You struggle to sleep; insomnia and other sleep disorders keep you awake at night, so you wake up more high-strung than before.

- You try to avoid situations, events, and people that make you nervous and trigger your anxious disposition.

- You are constantly dealing with digestive problems, stomach flu, etc.

- No matter how much you rest, you can't get over feeling fatigued and exhausted most of the time.

- You cannot focus on work, studies, or your daily chores because of the constant worry that works like a block to stop you from functioning normally.

In considering these symptoms, healthcare professionals can diagnose mental health disorders by categorizing them according to the severity of their symptoms. Let's look at modern society's most diagnosed anxiety disorders.

Types of Mental Disorders Connected to Anxiety

1. Agoraphobia

Panic rules this anxiety disorder, causing the person with agoraphobia to avoid events, situations, or places that cause them distress and a general feeling of nervousness. You fear embarrassment and a kind of suffocation as though you are trapped in a situation. You fear the lack of an escape route in these situations where you may be unable to "get away" when the fight or flight sensation of anxiety takes over. A few examples of such cases and places include:

- Being stuck in a crowd

- Panicking when confined in a small space or when you feel exposed in a large area.

- Having to be in a long queue with people milling all around you that you worry the situation may trigger a panic attack and you have no escape routes.

The flight or fight situation I mentioned before is an automatic reflex of your anxiety triggered by a panic attack. It is the reflex to flee from the situation or place rather than face a confrontation. The reaction occurs when adrenaline, a neurotransmitter, is secreted, which is responsible for causing your heart rate to increase, preparing you to flee.

Naturally, this reaction will sharpen your reflexes and prepare you to face danger. Still, when prone to panic attacks, this reaction is triggered inappropriately, causing distress in a normal situation.

Uncompounded fears can cause agoraphobia, such as the following:

- Fear of getting infected by a deadly virus if you leave your house and expose yourself to other people.

- Leaving the safety of your home can place you in harm's way, such as falling victim to a terrorist attack or getting caught by a bomb.

- Making a fool of yourself by behaving in a manner that will cause you embarrassment. The ridicule you think you will face is generally irrational and only manifested in your head.

2. **Anxiety that develops due to other medical reasons**

Physical health problems can cause anxiety disorders to manifest in some patients. Feelings of overwhelming dread, panic, and unease lead to anxiety disorders. A root cause of these symptoms is stress.

Medical conditions can cause severe stress and panic where the patient fears the unknown outcome they are facing. Living with a life-threatening disease can take a considerable toll on a patient's mind and lead to the development of anxiety brought on by panic and stress.

Research reveals a strong connection between people dealing with medical conditions and a rise in anxiety-related disorders within modern society (Aquin et al., 2017). However, most people are first diagnosed with anxiety because of the external symptoms the condition displays and only later found out to be dealing with a medical condition, which was the underlying cause of the anxiety in the first place.

Let's take panic attacks as an example. They display similar symptoms to a heart attack; palpitations, difficulty breathing, feelings of losing control, chest pain, and numbness. Hence, a health caregiver must be able to arrive at an accurate diagnosis of whether the anxiety stems from a medical disease or not. To do this, you may sometimes have to undergo further testing to determine the root cause of the mental health disorder.

Common medical conditions linked to anxiety disorders include the following.

- Hyperthyroidism and hypothyroidism result from an overactive or underactive thyroid gland.

- Hypoglycemia is often caused by diabetes and a drop in your blood glucose levels.

- Cardiac problems. Arrhythmia or congestive heart failure.

- Hyperventilation, pneumonia, and other illnesses or syndromes causing breathing difficulties.

3. **Generalized Anxiety Disorder (GAD)**

Continuous worry that revolves around several lifestyle factors is how GAD is classified. If you suffer from this anxiety disorder, you probably worry most of the time about every random aspect of your life. Your focus will keep shifting between different concerns. It might be your finances, health, family, children's education, career, and various other reasons that create worry, thus causing most women to stay up at night mulling over the consequences of dealing with all that worry-related stress.

Sometimes that worry is over issues that do not deserve that much attention and disturbance in the first place. If you have GAD, you will take those simple everyday worries and blow them out of proportion—making a mountain out of a molehill until you are mentally and physically tired and irritable. That type of worry sneaks up on you, piling up one by one until anxiety becomes a part of your everyday life, but you still cannot give it a proper reason for being there.

GAD is the most commonly diagnosed anxiety disorder among adults in the U.S., but the reason why most people develop GAD is not fully established; possible causes include:

- Biological reasons for developing GAD are sometimes linked to genetics, suggesting it may be an inherited condition because the likelihood of people dealing with GAD having a history of family members dealing with similar mental health disorders is high (McLaughlin et al., 2008). However, while genes may be a substantial cause for the inheritance of GAD, environmental influences remain the most probable cause for people developing generalized anxiety conditions.

- Experiencing an especially traumatic life event could also be another possibility; domestic violence or abuse, child abuse, bullying, a prolonged illness, or being witness to a particularly violent act are possible causes that may lead to GAD.

- Substance abuse, smoking, drugs, and alcohol are all triggers.

- Gender plays a key role as women are twice as likely to be diagnosed than men. Some of the reasons behind this statement are linked to a woman's fluctuating hormone levels causing mood changes and worry triggers. Plus, the possibility of women being more willing to seek help and receive a proper diagnosis is also a reason for the recorded numbers of people dealing with GAD being higher among the female population.

Most people dealing with GAD find it tough to get through the day. They face numerous and constant worries over mundane events or actions and have the persistent feeling of not being in control of their lives.

However, those diagnosed with moderate symptoms will continue to function, dealing with their turmoil internally while masking it from others. Such people will be socially active and maintain successful careers and lifestyles. Still, constant fear, doubt, and panic will prevail, holding them back from participating in specific events and avoiding situations they fear will trigger their panic attacks and anxiety.

Treatment is often successful, and one can manage GAD without profound implications. Seeking help promptly will prevent anxiety disorders from becoming more serious conditions such as depression, which can be treated or managed at a higher level than GAD.

4. **Panic disorder**

Experiencing more than one panic attack where suddenly you feel as though the world is closing in and you are suddenly overwhelmed by everything that you must flee is what is diagnosed as a panic disorder. A panic attack is a syndrome related to clinical anxiety and will have you worried and stressed over situations—even when you are in no real danger. Your behavior will be one of avoidance where you make it your mission to not fall into a similar situation as the one that already caused your panic attack. Therefore, you will go to great lengths to avoid specific circumstances.

In the U.S., at least one adult between the ages of 15 and 25 will experience a panic attack: statistically, about one in every ten people. Women are more susceptible to the attacks.

The most prevalent symptom of a panic attack is an overwhelming fear that takes place without any warning. It can happen anywhere at any moment because of a simple trigger. That fear is often accompanied by four or more of these symptoms.

- Sudden and excessive sweating

- Uncontrollable trembling

- Heart palpitations

- Sudden feelings of suffocation, followed by shortness of breath

- A choking sensation and a tightening of the throat

- Tightening of the chest accompanied by pain

- Nausea, stomach pain or cramps, and headaches

- Feeling faint

- Experiencing sudden chills or hot flashes

- Feeling disjointed, or not all there as though you are in a surreal situation, or you may feel like you are not in control of your mind

- Experiencing a sudden fear of death

Panic attacks often occur due to extreme stress and low self-esteem, where you are often left to fight negative emotions. Although suspected, a genetic link to panic attacks is not adequately established. Other reasons for someone experiencing a panic attack may be due to the following:

- As an underlying cause of depression

- Seasonal depression is an anxiety disorder that crops up during the winter when more people feel isolated and alone during the holidays, aggravated by the weather.

- Excessive consumption of alcohol and excessive smoking

- Harboring suicidal thoughts for which help has not been sought.

Because panic attacks display similar symptoms to heart attacks, extensive examinations should be performed by your healthcare provider to rule out possible underlying causes. You may be diagnosed with a panic disorder if you test negative for any physical ailments but have already experienced more than one panic attack.

5. **Separation anxiety disorder**

Contrary to what you may think, separation anxiety is not limited to a child's trauma when separated from a loved one. Indeed, separation anxiety is a natural process that very young children experience, starting from around the age of six months up to about three years, as a natural learning curve. But if those separation anxieties persist for longer, those children will be diagnosed as dealing with a child separation anxiety disorder.

Adults experience separation anxiety on a very distressing level; it's connected to feelings of extreme fear over the uncompounded dread of losing a loved one, together with the sense of doom as though something terrible is going to occur. Separation anxiety has no established cause but may be linked to other mental health disorders such as GAD, panic disorder, and agoraphobia.

While a child experiencing separation anxiety will fear detachment from their parents or primary caregivers, adults dealing with the syndrome will feel apprehension and fear of being separated from their loved ones. As a result, such individuals often end up unproductive in the workplace and cannot function efficiently even at other times as their minds cannot focus on their tasks.

The stresses that lead to someone developing the disorder may be the sudden loss of a loved one, adult children moving out of their family homes, and a particularly anxious individual having to travel for an extended time away from their homes. Other reasons linked to someone developing separation anxiety disorder are growing up among overbearing parents or even dealing with child separation anxiety in their younger years.

Diagnosed with disorders such as GAD, panic disorder, PTSD, and personality disorders puts you at risk of developing a separation anxiety disorder.

Symptoms of separation anxiety disorder

- Not being able to accept sleeping away from a loved one because you fear something bad will happen to them in your absence.

- A constant fear that has no real root cause, that harm will befall you or a loved one; in this case, the fear of abduction is highly prevalent.

- Not wanting to let a loved one out of sight, fearing your departure may cause harm to come upon them.

- Dealing with heightened depression due to the trauma experienced from bearing the burden of the above symptoms.

- Physical symptoms too can manifest as a result of adult separation anxiety, where you will feel actual pain in the form of stomach aches, headaches, and even an upset stomach.

Diagnosing separation anxiety disorder often happens by linking the symptoms to another anxiety disorder and making sure the symptoms have persisted for at least six months.

6. Social anxiety disorder

This disorder can be described as a social phobia where nervousness and butterflies in the stomach take the symptoms up a couple of notches to an extremely uncomfortable level.

Take the case of having to give a presentation to an audience. Most of us feel nervous and a bit anxious at having to do so, but when the time comes to make that presentation, we get on with it and get over it. However, dealing with a social anxiety disorder, you will suffer more deeply by becoming extremely anxious and nervous at the impending presentation.

You will experience embarrassment and heightened levels of anxiety and panic. You become painfully self-aware because you *think* you are being minutely scrutinized and judged for flaws and mistakes; therefore, you desperately fear making a blunder and feeling embarrassed in front of an audience.

Please do not confuse this disorder with the usual shyness that can often occur due to someone being taken out of their comfort zone, especially children. How comfortable a person feels in a social situation will depend on their personality. Some people are different. Some people are naturally shy and will be more reserved. That is no reason to identify them as having a social anxiety disorder. Other more profound symptoms lead to the diagnosis I have listed next.

- Constant and heightened fears that you are being observed in a negative light by others.

- An overwhelming worry that you are bound to cause embarrassment or become a social outcast because of your actions—those "actions" are only your thoughts, and the persistent self-doubt that somehow manages to convince you is a reality.

- An almost paralyzing fear at having to interact with strangers while feeling distressed that other people will notice your nervousness and introverted behavior.

- You are obsessed with the dread of making mistakes, looking foolish, and embarrassing yourself, and so you tend to avoid interacting with others as much as possible.

- You avoid attracting attention and prefer to be invincible; you dread being in the spotlight.

- Self-judgment is high, and you are your worst critic, constantly analyzing your actions and finding flaws. ("I could have done better")

- Always being negative and expecting the worst from every situation, where you harbor negative thoughts like these—I am simply not likable enough or popular enough to make a good impression. People are merely friendly because they feel sorry for me and not because they like me.

- You fear others will notice your physical symptoms of awkwardness, such as blushing or excessive sweating.

Physical Symptoms of Dealing with a Social Phobia

Some people experience physically manifested symptoms when faced with an uncomfortable situation where they feel anxious or embarrassed. You could demonstrate such signs if you are dealing with a social phobia and can include the following:

- A heightened heart rate

- Excessive sweating

- Flushed cheeks where you suddenly feel the heat rise in your face, and you dread others noticing it.

- Nausea and feeling as though you are going to vomit, and even sudden diarrhea that crops up.

- Your muscles start to tense, and your experience stomach cramps

- You feel as though you can't breathe

- Your mind suddenly goes blank

Everyday situations you will try to avoid because of your social anxiety disorder

- You try to avoid social gatherings and shy away from parties or other social gatherings where you feel vulnerable and timid.

- You dread making an entrance to a place where the others have already gathered as you fear your entry will be evident since everyone else is probably already seated.

- You avoid making eye contact when talking to people or, in general, avoid holding eye contact or looking away too soon.

- You feel awkward going on dates because you are tense and cannot relax

- You dislike having to engage in conversations and try to avoid such situations

- You feel nervous eating in front of other people and tend to feel very self-conscious and clumsy.

- You dread having to take back a purchase you need to return because you then must deal with explanations; you try to avoid having to deal with strangers as much as possible.

What are the Causes of Social Phobia?

Like many mental health disorders, environmental factors mainly cause social phobias. Genetics plays a minor role among some people who seem to have inherited the condition with a family history of mental health disorders.

Children with overprotective and controlling parents or those who observe similar anxious behavior in their parents or caregivers are more likely to develop the condition. Because there are suspicions that social anxiety disorders which are a person's personality or characteristics are a type of disorder that someone can pick up by emulating others. Social phobias are some of the more manageable mental health disorders to overcome and are highly responsive to the methods I will introduce in the upcoming chapters.

7. **Substance-induced anxiety disorders**

Several substances can interfere with your brain's chemicals that control your moods, thoughts, and behavior. Neurotransmitters and hormones secrete chemicals that govern various aspects of your behavior.

The amygdala in your brain is one of the systems that govern the secretion of neurotransmitters and hormones controlling your emotions and thoughts. Its function can sometimes make you feel off-balanced when certain substances cause interference, the most noted include the following:

- Alcohol

- Over-the-counter medication such as decongestants

- Illegal drugs cocaine, LSD

- Some types of diet pills

- Certain medications prescribed for attention deficit disorders, Parkinson's, stimulants, and steroids

Some medications and substances will cause anxiety syndromes while taking them. In contrast, others may affect you adversely and cause stress and anxiety after you stop taking them if you become dependent on the mood alterations they provide, which leads to substance abuse.

Symptoms of substance-induced anxiety disorders include the following:

- Becoming paranoid and being on edge all the time, expecting something terrible to take place at any moment

- Dealing with insomnia and other sleep disorders that prevent you from enjoying a good night's sleep

- Losing your appetite or developing stomach pains that will lead to weight loss

- Loss of focus, becoming forgetful

- Feeling dizzy, getting the shakes

- Heart palpitations, hot flushes, feeling numb and sweating excessively

- Struggling to stay in control and feeling as though you are losing your mind

- Thinking that you are going to die

If you develop substance-induced anxiety, you must be completely honest about what you have been ingesting. Prescription drugs, illegal drugs, alcohol, etcetera, be precise about how much and how often you take the substances that have led to your condition. Based on the information you provide, your healthcare worker will be able to make an accurate diagnosis and prescribe a path to recovery. Anyone diagnosed with an anxiety disorder before taking the substances that can induce additional anxiety symptoms will not be diagnosed as dealing with substance-induced anxiety.

Causes of Anxiety

Although the exact causes of anxiety are yet to be discovered, some factors have been identified as triggers for mental health diseases. We explored a few under each syndrome; now, let's take a more comprehensive look at each one of the known causes that lead to anxiety syndromes.

1. **Medical conditions that cause anxiety**

   - Several medical conditions that induce stress and worry are linked to the patient sometimes developing an anxiety condition.

   - Heart disease

   - Irritable bowel syndrome (IBS)

   - Thyroid problems

   - Diabetes

   - Asthma and other respiratory illnesses

   - Addiction to banned substances

   - Withdrawal symptoms caused by an addiction to alcohol or antidepressant drugs

   - Tumors that can trigger anxiety and mood changes

2. **Family history of mental health diseases**

Some types of anxiety disorders may be inherited. This is especially true among people with a family history of mental health diseases, although genetics is not a leading cause of anxiety.

The percentage of inheriting an anxiety disorder is 30%, with a 44% probability of inheriting panic disorders and 39% for agoraphobia (Villafuerte & Burmeister, 2003).

The more likely reason genetics play a role in mental health disorders is suspected to be gene inheritance and, with it, a heritage of personality traits. Those traits can be the root cause of some people developing anxiety disorders rather than a gene containing the condition itself being passed down along the generations.

Personality traits identified as being more susceptible to developing anxiety include the following:

- People with non or very low self-esteem

- Timid individuals

- People who are easily confused or get upset

- Those who strive to be perfectionists

- People who want to be in control find any situations that prevent them from doing so quite stressful. That type of personality trait often leads to an individual being high-strung and anxious.

Children who display these conditions are at a higher risk of developing anxiety later due to their inherited personality traits.

3. Personality traits

Personality traits causing anxiety certainly deserve to be explored more. A state of tension, being nervous most of the time, and being too timid are all characteristics that encourage a build-up of stress, resentment, and anxiety. Let's put some personality traits prone to anxiety into perspective to see if you can identify with any of them.

- Harboring a resistance to change

A decisive factor associated with anxiety is the fear of change. People diagnosed with the syndrome are quite averse to changing routines and losing what is familiar. They rely on familiarity to keep their worries at bay and see a change in a negative light that takes them out of their comfort zone. People displaying resistance to change as a personality trait are highly susceptible to developing anxiety syndromes at a later stage.

- Being an overthinker

Are you one? Or do you know one? Either way, you know how stressful being an overthinker can be. Overthinking and over-analyzing your actions, the actions, and the intentions of others can take quite a toll on your mind. You not only analyze what people say and do, but you start to arrive at conclusions that are not pretty, and which may be harmful to your inner peace and sense of self-worth and increase your stress levels.

- Chasing perfectionism

The need to do everything perfectly is perfectionism that leads to anxiety. The desire to achieve perfection in everything you do and spending more time than is necessary on tasks perfecting them is stressful. It can easily lead to anxiety disorders because you constantly worry about inadequacies. Due to this type of worry, the stress of perfectionism often evolves into a social anxiety syndrome of GAD.

- A lack of patience

Constantly getting irritated and displaying impatience can lead to anxiety. Being irritable means you are dealing with mood shifts most of the time. You lack patience and are quick to get angry. Both are traits that can lead to elevated blood pressure levels. The mind fills with anxiety as you view everything with trepidation and doubt as if you are waiting to be disappointed and let down, leading to an excuse to vent your frustrations.

- Too much empathy

In short, being a pushover is not healthy in the long run. Quite often, people with too much empathy toward others end up bearing quite a load in terms of stress and anxiety. They are often taken advantage of and perform thankless favors that build up tension and resentment.

- Choosing to avoid dealing with problems or situations

Avoidance is a common trait associated with anxiety. Most people diagnosed with the condition prefer to avoid situations, events, places, and even people that make them anxious and fearful of triggering their panic and stress. Avoidance behavior is a good reflection of how someone with anxiety tries to hide away from society and remain in their comfort zone. Having a personality trait where you try to avoid leaving your comfort zone and thereby avoiding situations and people can become stressful and lead to the development of anxiety conditions, which sadly only strengthens that personality trait.

4. **Career and workplace-related anxiety issues**

Just about anyone can relate to a job-related problem, and indeed work-related stress is the second highest in the U.S. Let's look at the statistics according to the Centers for Diseases Control (CDC):

- The number of people reporting an extremely stressful job—is 40%. One-fourth of employed people in the U.S. claim that the primary source of stress they deal with is their job.

- The numbers that claim jobs stress interferes with family

life—26% (CDC, 1999)

Most people claim an increase in job stress over the last generation, and indeed job stress today is a marker for several mental and physical conditions. Heart diseases, the development of musculoskeletal disorders, and psychological conditions, among which suicide is listed as a probability, although more research is still underway. The bottom line is that work-related stress is extremely unhealthy and damaging to your mental and physical health.

Anxiety and burnout are linked to job stress and are markers for developing mental health disorders. Working that extra hour at the office can lead to unhealthy lifestyle habits, missing out on your lunch, or not getting enough sleep. Stressful working environments lead to low self-esteem and mood fluctuations that can follow you back home. Stress can affect your family, leaving you even more distressed over your uncontrolled emotions. Work stress can build up and suddenly become an anxiety-related condition, together with depression and other forms of anxiety attacks. Job stress can be extremely harmful to women juggling multiple roles and dealing with several anxiety issues domestically and at the workplace.

5. **Stress caused by family and relationship problems**

Being in a relationship or managing a family can be challenging, and stress and anxiety play a big part. Several factors cause disruptions leading to stress and anxiety within a relationship or family unit: arguments, distrust, a lack of support, no proper compromise or give-and-take scenario, and uncertainty. Such factors can cause a division among the strongest bonds.

The rat race or the stresses of modern lifestyles heavily influence anxiety syndromes related to personal issues. Endless to-do lists, a lack of enough quality time to spend with family, health problems, and exhaustion are reasons your personal life is causing your anxiety. It does not mean that your relationship or family is different or worse than others. Such issues are common among most families and partners. The difference is how the problems are handled.

6. **Emotional or physical abuse**

Trauma is a huge trigger for anxiety and can take many shapes. Abusive relationships are one of the leading causes of trauma-related anxiety; an abusive relationship is not always physical. Words and actions that do not lay a hand on a person can hurt them more deeply, scarring them and leaving a mental mark that overshadows most of their life's decisions, future goals, successes, and happiness.

Emotional abuse is not talked about as much as violent domestic abuse, but sadly it is just as severe and damaging. Most often, people in an emotionally abusive relationship are not aware of how much hurt they are causing each other. As you would have realized by now, anxiety syndromes creep up on you over time. It is not like the flu or a headache you suddenly endure and then feel better; anxiety builds up blow by blow and will culminate in an awful episode that leaves you vulnerable and unsure about how to act.

Emotional abuse is the same; it starts affecting your self-esteem, confidence, and courage until you suddenly realize you are devoid of all identity and self-worth. Negative actions, guilt-tripping, and putting down your partner to control, scare, hurt, or manipulate them is how emotional abuse works.

Obvious Emotional Abuse Tactics

You will be surprised to realize that you may be under the influence of some of these actions without realizing that you are dealing with a form of emotional abuse. Can you identify with any of them?

- You have a partner used to putting you down with little hurtful statements that may seem inconsequential. Still, they make you feel low and unappreciated, belittling you, shaming you, making you feel unattractive, telling you you are incompetent, etc.

- Threatening suicide or similar ultimatum to get you to agree, comply or give up a goal, ambition, or new move to leave a toxic relationship.

- Manipulating you; lies, threats, guilt trips, gaslighting

- Behaving in a threatening manner to instill fear

Subtle Emotional Abuse Tactics

Sometimes emotional abuse takes place without the victim realizing they are being manipulated. Giving in to the needs of the manipulative partner takes place because the victim feels empathy, guilt, and love and does not want to cause hurt. Still, they do not realize the enormous emotional turmoil they bear due to being suppressed and made to live life according to someone else's needs and rules. Can you identify with any of these subtle signs of emotional abuse?

- Threatening to walk out or drive away during an argument that crops up regarding a disagreement.

- Giving you the silent treatment, which can be traumatic, makes you feel isolated, lonely, and confused.

- Restricting your interactions with the opposite sex because of jealousy or not trusting you.

- Spying on you by keeping a tab of your whereabouts and checking your phone or laptop.

- Frequent displays of jealousy may seem flattering but soon evolve into a red flag where you must display caution and curtail your friendships with people of the opposite sex. You might feel you have to hold back on your promotion at work or salary increments if the jealousy stems from a feeling of inadequacy.

- Holding you accountable for any misfortune or problems in the relationship or family, as though it was all your fault.

Emotional abuse puts you in a very vulnerable and mentally unstable state. You are constantly trying to please your partner and prevent triggers that get the abuse going. You lose your self-confidence and live an unhappy life, thus bearing a considerable burden while dealing with trauma, stress, and anxiety.

Chronic stress is often a result of emotional abuse. Other effects include developing high functioning anxiety, PTSD, clinical depression, insomnia, feelings of frustration, helplessness, anger, and even resorting to substance abuse.

7. Enduring emotional neglect during childhood

A child who is neglected emotionally by their parents or caregiver often grows up feeling very insecure and with low self-esteem. Emotional neglect happens over time when a child's primary caregivers regularly fail to meet their emotional needs. Not responding immediately to a picture their child drew is not emotional neglect.

As parents, only some can give their children 100% of their attention all the time. Suppose they don't make up for time away from attending to their child's needs and avoid bonding, nurtur-ing, motivational pep talks, or reassuring their child's emotional insecurities. In that case, they will not meet their child's emotional needs.

Not acknowledging a child's emotions and reacting negatively to them, shaming them, and being aloof are all forms of emotional neglect created as a pattern and standard behavior of parents unable to care for their children's emotional needs.

You would probably deal with anxiety-related syndromes if you grew up under such circumstances.

- A lack of self-esteem

- Not finding a connection in your relationships

- Dissociating yourself most of the time

- A limited vocabulary when it comes to expressing feelings

- Feeling uncomfortable when it comes to emotional ex-pressions

- Being extremely sensitive toward rejection

- A high risk of developing an anxiety disorder

Emotional distancing is naturally present in people without strong emotional bonding with their caregivers since children learn emo-tional expressions by emulating their primary caregivers.

8. **Post-traumatic anxiety disorders**

Anxious thoughts, emotions, and behavior can prevail in adult-hood, with childhood trauma as a root cause. Witnessing or expe-riencing a traumatic childhood event can damage a young mind. It is difficult to overcome without proper therapy to heal, even at a later stage. Adult children who are trauma victims will continue to endure flashbacks and the mental agony of the event from time to time.

Neglect, abuse, and abandonment that require adult rationale and skills to deal with can be overwhelming for children. As a result, they may develop anxious thoughts and find themselves confused and dealing with pain and guilt because they feel they are to be blamed for their situation.

Likewise, adults dealing with anxiety syndromes due to childhood trauma may display a helpless nature, a reflection of the trauma they went through during their childhood and not one that accurately reflects their weaknesses and natural abilities. Projecting themselves as vulnerable is a projection of the distress and feelings of helplessness they experienced as children.

9. **Other causes of anxiety—grief, social exclusion, and being bullied**

Grieving the loss of a loved one is natural and can be heightened if it is a parent or someone you were close to and with whom you had a strong bond. That said, it is unnatural to continue to grieve excessively about six months after the passing of a loved one. Such extended grief could indicate an anxiety syndrome brought on by an event that was too traumatic for you to process.

Social isolation is highly prevalent in this time of social media, where everyone is connected—virtually. Human beings are social creatures, and we need to interact with others, not through "likes" or "thumbs up," but through physical interactions; laughing, talking, and enjoying each other's company face to face is essential.

Sadly, in an era where the importance of cultivating an inclusive society is highlighted, most of us live in isolation. Such loneliness can lead to anxiety and the development of social phobias.

Social exclusion is a culprit where people are labeled according to their race, gender, sexual orientation, and other factors; experiencing alienation based on the labels allocated to us is one of the most distressing actions for the mind to bear.

Exclusion on these grounds can take many forms; verbal abuse, being made to feel like an outcast and "other," as is often the case in gender-identity-based biases, characteristics that society deems undesirable or unacceptable, a person's social standing, and judgmental thinking are some. Withdrawal is a symptom of social exclusion.

You can overcome the trauma of social exclusion by seeking out and forming relationships with people not committed to following the rules of social exclusion. And by not striving to "fit in" but embracing your individuality and joining support groups to strengthen your resolve to stop being affected by social stigmas.

The techniques I will introduce in the following chapters will help you strengthen those resolutions and overcome hurtful and stressful actions through exercises to make your mind stronger, thus becoming self-aware and confident.

The Light at the end of the Dark Tunnel—Hope

Most anxiety disorders are highly treatable, and no one needs to suffer in silence. Reaching out for help will give you access to several resources. Being open and accepting your condition and need for help is the first step. The techniques and resources I will introduce in the following chapters will help you obtain clarity and a stronger resolve to fight your anxiety. However, some conditions and situations need further analysis and a proper medical diagnosis; therefore, if your anxiety symptoms are severe, you should visit your healthcare provider for an appropriate assessment.

How Can Anxiety Be Treated?

- Counseling and therapy

- Medical diagnosis and medication

- Mindfulness meditation practices and meditation

- Physical activity/exercise

- Lifestyle changes include assessing one's diet, sleeping habits, socialization practices, etc.

- Grounding techniques. This method distracts your anxious thoughts; tools such as sound, sight, and smell are used to create distractions whenever anxiety, such as panic disorders, takes over. I will explain more about the use and benefits of grounding techniques in chapter 5.

Anxiety Doesn't Choose

A mental health syndrome affects people regardless of who they are. Wealth, social standing, popularity, etc., are all irrelevant factors when it comes to anxiety; the condition can strike anyone as a culmination of stressful events, inherited characteristics, or the impact of one traumatic episode. What's important is the need to heal, and because anxiety is a condition of the mind, you can learn to reset your thoughts, decompress, and reduce the stressors, and avoid triggers. That is what "Controlling Anxiety" is based on, and I am very excited to start chapter 2, where we unveil anxiety, so you may see it is not the monster you perceive it to be, not if you choose for it not to be so.

Use the focus journal in chapter 10 to transfer your thoughts to a source outside of your mind, thus preventing yourself from suffocating as your anxious thoughts come tumbling down one after another. Use the worksheets I provided to coincide with techniques discussed in the book to find answers to your questions and decipher the root cause of your anxieties and their severity.

CHAPTER 2

— • —

GOOD VS. BAD

*D*octors, counselors, saying there's something

wrong with me.

My parents telling me to calm down and stop being so crazy.

But how can I calm down when the world around me

is spinning out of control and I can barely see?

Breathe. You will get through this. —Tiffaney L Ganci (Ganci, 2018)

In chapter 1, I told you about anxiety working as a defense mechanism to keep your ancestors alive. It was a nervous tension caused by anxiety that kept them on alert and ready to face danger at any given moment. That is the true function of anxiety; it is not the monster our modern lifestyles have made it out to be. There are many times that anxiety would have come to your rescue. In this chapter, we will look at the two faces of anxiety, the good and the bad, because to conquer, you must know the true nature of your enemy and whether your enemy set out to cause you harm.

Demi Lovato—Champions Accepting Yourself for Who You Are!

Demi Lovato embraces her anxiety and has turned an otherwise traumatic condition into a positive reason for helping others like her. Debunking any myths that make anxiety seem like a condition to hide, Demi advocates being open about her anxiety and does not try to hide her eating disorder. The singer, who is an advocate for body positivity, has revealed her love for stuffed toys which she says is her coping mechanism against loneliness and panic attacks.

Demi uses her knowledge and experience with mental health disorders to help others like her overcome the stigma and seek answers. She is strong enough to accept and smart enough to turn to coping mechanisms, even if it is as simple as a child's toy. Are you ready to understand, accept and start healing from your anxiety? Let's look at anxiety in a different light.

What is Good Anxiety? A Misunderstood Feeling?

To understand the good side of anxiety, you need to look at anxiety as your protective tool. It keeps you safe, instilling a percentage of panic, doubt, caution, and fear when making certain decisions, being in an uncomfortable situation, etcetera. Anxiety raises red flags to make you aware of impending dangers.

Suppose you take out the anxiety component from your senses altogether. In that case, you will be walking around thinking everything is A-okay all the time, a fine state of being until something goes drastically wrong, and you wonder why you did not sense any danger. You would have no doubts when making decisions, and quite often, doubts help you to weigh the pros and cons of a situation before deciding. You would not be able to sense danger in a place or person without a certain level of anxiety because anxious thoughts often crop up when you are not comfortable with a situation. Bottom line: You need a certain amount of anxiety to keep you safe.

How Do I Embrace Good Anxiety?

Now that you know not all anxiety is bad let's look at methods to make maximum use of anxiety for your benefit. To begin, you must change the relationship you have cultivated with anxiety; it must be one of mutual benefit and not of fear.

Let's look at creating that relationship in four easy steps.

1.Turn your thoughts into something productive.

Constant worry over mundane factors is part of your anxiety; worrying about all the chores you need to get done, the tasks you must finish at the office, and the responsibilities you need to meet will not go away. What you can do is make yourself a tidy little to-do list and schedule how you are going to get about getting the tasks completed.

Think of your anxiety as a very efficient secretary who keeps re-minding you of everything you need to do. Take those thoughts and turn them into productive little nudges that make you spring into action instead of letting your chores pile up, leading to con-stant worry, anxiety, and last-minute panic attacks.

2. Use your sensitivities to become sensitive toward others.

Empathy is another lesson you can learn from your anxiety. Your fears will serve as an insight into the type of stress that others are going through. No one will understand the pain of stress and the terror of a panic attack than you. Therefore, you should be able to connect and form a bond of understanding with others, whether they are dealing with anxiety or not, in situations that cause them distress. Being able to sympathize and show compassion because you understand the emotions someone is dealing with is a massive asset to being overly anxious.

Increased sensitivity and concern for others are common among people with anxiety disorders. One reason is rumination worry, and the need to be accepted, making you constantly concerned about the other person's feelings, thus increasing your sense of empathy.

Such traits are a plus point for you as an individual as you are then perceived as a caring type, a good friend, and a sympathetic listener; good qualities to possess and bestowed on you by anxiety.

What makes you highly sensitive to others' feelings is, in part, your insecurity and the constant worry of looking "bad" in front of others. Your anxiety causes a pang of hunger that makes you want to feel liked and accepted at all times. Use that overly sensitive nature for your benefit by turning it around to make you not a clingy and anxious individual but one that is sensitive to the needs of others and understanding on a personal level.

3. Become smarter and more informed

Anxiety keeps you alert and always looking for possible outcomes; your mind is constantly active, seeking answers and puzzling over questions. Those traits make a person dealing with anxiety much brighter than average. Using your cognitive skills to analyze, deduce and explore a range of scenarios, as is the case among people dealing with anxiety syndromes, is the main reason behind heightened intelligence.

Best of all, being smarter is more than a theory for people dealing with anxiety. Studies confirm that research conducted among people with GAD confirmed a connection between higher anxiety levels and increased intelligence (Coplan et al., 2012).

This happens because worry and anxiety cause activation of common neural links in your brain, which is the connection between your central nervous system responsible for your thoughts, actions, and behavior, your cognitive functions. Thus, scientists consider pathological anxiety (perceived as bad) a positive trait when it influences cognitive functions.

4. **Draw motivation from your anxiety**

Purpose anxiety is a syndrome that develops from the stress of not having a purpose in life and the quest to look for one. The two main factors contributing to anxiety are discovering your purpose in life and the pressure of trying to achieve that purpose. The anxiety that develops, as a result, will take several forms; fear, frustration, worry, and stress all culminate as anxiety that can range from moderate to severe.

The frustrations that build up and cause purpose anxiety to have their roots in feelings of inadequacy, not achieving satisfaction in life, such as constantly changing jobs and not being able to settle on a single purpose in life.

But what if you take that constant hunger and feelings of inadequacy and turn them around from causing anxiety to causing motivation?

As you can see, anxiety has several plus factors that shine a light on its true purpose: to act as a protective mechanism to keep you alert to dangers or threats. However, sadly, the stresses of modern living have turned what is a natural safety reflex into one that garners fear, frustrations, and caution. A "syndrome" that needs treatment.

When Anxiety Turns Bad!

We have already explored different types of anxiety and their symptoms; therefore, I will not dwell on anxiety and what it is. Instead, I would like to help you recognize the instances when anxiety turns bad when it changes from being a protective mechanism to one that can cause grievous harm.

To realize a build-up of anxiety, you must be able to recognize the signs when worry turns to stress, panic, and a whole lot of anxious thoughts. We all worry at some point in our lives, perhaps even several times a day; that is anxiety's protective mechanism kicking in. We use those pockets of worry as warning signals to re-think, not go ahead with an action or decision and even stay away from certain situations and individuals. Many people call it their sixth sense, but your anxiety is trying to protect you.

When usual bouts of worry start to remain long after the threat has passed, making you nervous and panicky most of the day, you begin to worry about fundamental concerns more intensely than you should. That indicates that everything is not okay with your protective mechanism; it is not functioning as it should and suggests that you are on the verge of or already dealing with an anxiety-related condition.

Let's look at typical anxiety symptoms that can turn bad.

- The severity of your worry goes from basic fear and anxiety to rumination worry, which is constant negative thinking and is highly disruptive, as it interferes with your daily functions. The increased severity of your anxiety becomes an emotion/mood that warrants an assessment; it is no longer a normal worry and has changed from being a protective mechanism to one that is unsettling and hard to bear.

- The length of time your worry lasts becomes longer. Your anxiety or worry does not disappear with the threat as normal worry that suddenly crops up does. We generally worry about an event and then forget about it and move on to other emotions once the reason for the concern is sorted. But when anxiety is bad, that worry continues as a baseless negative thought or feeling. And it can even crop up for no valid reason when there is no real threat.

- Bad anxiety interferes with your daily functions and disrupts your lifestyle. Nothing feels the same; worry, negativity, doubt, fear, and panic are dominant emotions most of the time—for no apparent reason.

- You start to fear events, feelings, or actions that you are beginning to recognize as triggers for your sudden anxiety because they can set off your panic attacks and other anxiety symptoms.

- Your life worsens, and anxiety creates problems for you. Trying to avoid triggers is one of the most significant trials, especially if you are dealing with a social phobia where avoiding people and being out in public soon starts to have unsavory effects on your lifestyle and overall well-being. You face isolation and a loss of contact as though you no longer belong in society.

Let me end this chapter by reiterating the importance of turning the tables and using your anxious behavior for your benefit. Being alert to the changes that are taking place in your mind and body will help you to become sensitive to your sudden emotional shifts. A beneficial method for knowing when you need to turn to the comfort of a coping mechanism to help deal with your anxiety. And that is what my next chapter is about, battling and conquering your mind's worst enemy—overthinking. Let's look at the available weapons.

CHAPTER 3

— • —

CONQUER OVERTHINKING

*Y*ou will get through the sleepless nights,

all the internal fights,

and the days that seem right

when the world hits you with all its might.

Breathe. You will get through this. —Tiffaney L Ganci (Ganci, 2018)

Overthinking is the root of all anxious thoughts. The what if's, why, how, and when are at the base of all doubt, panic, terror, and fear that make up anxiety syndromes. You will learn to conquer your anxious thoughts in this chapter because that is something you can do. You did not know how to until now. So, get ready to "breathe" and get through those "constant internal fights," otherwise known as overthinking.

It's All About Emotional Control Shawn Mendes Style

Let's start this chapter with inspiration from Grammy Award winner Shawn Mendes. He has recently battled with anxiety and is not afraid to accept his emotional vulnerabilities while making a considerable effort to get his emotions under control. And he is succeeding and starting to radiate a positive vibe that shows the mind is stronger than we think.

The young artist explains he was under intense anxiety, which at one time prevented him from singing as the physical symptoms of his mental health disorder manifested in his throat, causing a blockage. Never a quitter, Shawn decided to fight his emotional state and turned to a personal coach for guidance. He practiced control and conquered overthinking through daily meditation sessions and breathing exercises, and guess what? He imposed a social media ban until 11 a.m. each day. The singer states his success in taking control of his anxieties relies on his determination to take control of and become accountable for his thoughts and mental health and the direction they take daily. Holding yourself responsible for your thoughts and preventing overthinking is what this chapter is all about. If you can draw strength and inspiration from Shawn Mendes, following the techniques I have outlined here will be a success (Nast, 2021).

What Is Overthinking?

We are all accused of overthinking at some point or the other—especially women! "You are overthinking the issue." is probably a sentence you are familiar with, but what exactly does it mean to overthink?

Unproductive thoughts that go deeper than necessary and seem on a continuous loop contribute to the term "overthinking." In a nutshell, I am talking about rumination worry, a negative pattern of anxious thoughts that ignite a constant worry. In conjunction with anxiety, overthinking is centered on worry that has no proper base. It is a worry that can have you stressing about the past and the future as well as the present. The impossibility of this type of thought structure that seems to be on a continuous loop has no solution. It is an exaggerated and baseless type of hopeless worry—overthinking and blowing your worry out of proportion.

Sadly, overthinking stems from one of our most vital and beneficial traits; the power our brains possess to handle different and complex thoughts simultaneously.

Overthinking is the same as anxiety. It is one of our protective mechanisms warning us about decisions or actions by making us think about the pros and cons of what we are about to do. It is that little nagging feeling in the back of your mind telling you to be cautious and think more deeply about what you are about to do.

However, this auto mechanism, which occurs when your mind starts analyzing several different thoughts (angles to a decision you are about to make), becomes your enemy when you begin to think beyond reason. Rumination worry steps in and takes over rational thinking. Otherwise, it is important to understand that overthinking is a protective mechanism that allows us to prepare for the future and establish fail-safe plans.

The reason anxiety turns into a mental health disorder is mainly due to constant worry, and that worry has its roots in overthinking. Just like worry that stems from anxiety is baseless and persistent, the rumination worry that causes overthinking on a constant rewind session is also baseless; a signal that all is not well with your mind.

You start to sabotage your relationships, career, and family life when you overthink your present situation. You see problems where there are none, eventually creating a situation that justifies your overthinking.

Perceive yourself in a negative light, and it is going to reflect on your overall well-being and quality of life. A mother who loses confidence in herself and sees herself as a failure will not be the inspiration and strength the family needs.

If you constantly worry about events that are yet to happen, whether they are short or long-term issues, you are setting yourself up to deal with overthinking about future events.

Can I Be Dealing with Overthinking Issues?

Your habit of overthinking happens automatically. Your brain is constantly making conscious and unconscious calls concerning your decisions. Overthinking may not raise red flags for you initially, and your analytical power will be perceived as a problem-solving ability or one that helps with self-reflection. However, there are limits to how far you can take both characteristics.

Suppose your problem-solving process continues after the problem. In that case, you may go into an endless worry about an event, dredging up the incident and refreshing it in your mind until you finally turn a minor matter into major anxiety for you—that is not problem-solving.

If your self-reflection becomes an obsession, it becomes self-derogatory. You indulge in negative self-talk and endlessly worry about an aspect of yourself that you are not able to change or control—beyond the normal parameters of self-reflection.

It's a fine line between being self-reflective or analytical—and overthinking. For most of us, the habit seems natural, and you simply label yourself a "worrier." That label may be accurate, except it is not something to be taken lightly because what you could be is a "chronic overthinker." Or a chronic worrier.

A chronic overthinker will go deeper than is natural into their thoughts, thus, experiencing stress and anxiety on many different levels. The condition will lead to sleep disruptions and affect your health, relationships, and work. Being a chronic overthinker prevents you from experiencing life the way you could; you become nervous, overly cautious, and doubtful about making decisions. You become obsessed with the past and fearful of the future until your anxious thoughts weaken your mind so that you cannot cope with life's daily stresses; each one seems doubly troubling and beyond a solution for you. This type of rumination worry is primarily fictional, but for you, it is genuine and damaging stress that never ends.

Here are some signs that could indicate you are an overthinker.

- Your mind hits the replay button for you to keep viewing specific incidents, often unpleasant, repeatedly. A lot of what-ifs and whys follow those reruns.

- Similar to rethinking incidents, you can't seem to stop thinking about past events/comments that are disturbing or stressful.

- You become obsessed with factors that are beyond your control.

- Rethinking conversations over and over, wondering and analyzing what people said and did.

- You are doubtful and constantly second-guess your decisions.

- You will envision and expect the worst outcomes.

- You even try to look for hidden meanings in what people said and did to try and justify your doubts and distrust of others.

- You stay up all night thinking about problems, or you may even wake up at odd hours and start worrying about past, present, or future events.

- You move your worries along into your future, turning a problem that can be resolved now into a long-term issue that you envision affecting your future. Or you connect to your past and keep rethinking events you have no control over.

Creating problems through overthinking and then linking them to past and future events can become highly stressful and result in you having to deal with mental and physical ailments. Depression, anxiety, and stress do not affect the mind alone; you can feel their effects physically.

- Extreme fatigue.

- Headaches that do not go away.

- A lack of concentration where your mind cannot focus on one task.

- Feeling nauseous and having appetite changes, you may suddenly lose your appetite or look for comfort in food by overeating.

- You develop sleep problems.

Left unchecked overthinking can do a lot of damage. Become more conscious of your thoughts and behavior. You must identify the times you go too deep into your head. When that realization hits you, stop—take a breather and rethink the anxiety and stress you are building over your obsessive analysis of a problem, event, action, or past conversation.

Accept and let go of problems you cannot change; instead, try to find other aspects in connection that you can manipulate to ease the situation for you—decide on letting go of overthinking thoughts for which you have no solution.

When Overthinking Turns into Negative Self-Talk and Anxiety

When you become your worst critic, it's hard to escape the constant negativity.

Dealing with anxious thoughts is challenging; you are constantly suspicious, stressed, and depressed about general issues. Plus, when you add negative self-talk to those anxieties, it becomes unbearable.

Have you ever stayed awake in the night, over-analyzing your behavior?

- Why did I end up partying so hard?

- Second guessing and questioning yourself—I should not have... or I could have... or what if I had not done...?

Those types of rumination worry will go on and on in an endless loop, making you feel inferior, a failure, and less confident. None of it is true though and comes from your negative self-talk. Therefore, you can stop that type of thinking and overcome your negativity to realize how special you are.

The negativity you are generating about yourself is a trigger that sets off your anxiety or may even lead to you developing anxiety syndrome. The more you encourage negative talk, the more power you give those anxieties to grow and fester. Once triggered, it's hard to overcome the panic and constant worry that follows. That worry also links your negative thoughts to past events, replaying the scenarios in your mind and making you sad, disappointed, and regrettable.

You do not deserve to put yourself through all that!

That type of negative self-talk is based on your thoughts with dire consequences.

- The more you keep telling yourself you are incapable of a particular action, the more convinced your mind becomes to think you are incapable of the action. It's as if your negative thought manifested itself into a reality.

- Your relationships start to suffer. You become increasingly dissatisfied, analyzing, and trying to find hidden meanings in what your partner or friends say or do. You become highly critical and overly expectant, anticipating the type of behavior you associate with the "perfect" relationship.

- You start wanting perfection. Good enough is simply no good anymore. You want things to be exceptional—perfect. You begin to dissect everything to try and zero in on what you believe needs fixing; you are no longer happy with being just a high achiever.

- Depression sets in because the pressure of constantly striving for perfection, analyzing relationships, and relentlessly criticizing yourself will certainly not leave much room for happy thoughts of self-satisfaction.

- You suffer from low self-esteem and may even indulge in behavior you regret later.

- Your mind and anxieties go beyond your control, and you become a prisoner of your negative thoughts.

As bleak and dark as negative self-talk sounds, you can teach yourself to overcome the habit of indulging in the behavior. But first, it's essential to understand why and what causes this type of negative behavior to manifest in the first place.

Why Do We Indulge in Pointing the Finger at Ourselves—The Root Cause of Negative Self-Talk

Emotions are hard to let go of; we need time to overcome disappointment or sadness when we get hurt. But out of all those emotions, the type that we find the most difficult to overcome is the self-derogatory feelings—guilt, blame, and shame. Such emotions remain like an unpleasant aftertaste in our minds until we can work through our thoughts and feelings to finally overcome the negativity.

Sadly, when negative self-talk is a dominant characteristic, emotions such as shame, guilt, overgeneralization of problems, and self-blame remain and fester, causing a substantial emotional wound. Let's not forget mislabeling, otherwise known as global labeling, which is a part of our modern society. It is the act of categorizing an individual, allocating their character to a label based on a one-sided analysis of who they are.

All these conditions, coupled with your constant lack of self-esteem, lead to negative self-talk—I am just not good enough because... (the reasons are endless, how many can you list?)

Those reasons are called cognitive distortions. A false perception of yourself becomes true—exaggerated thoughts that are not factual. Cognitive distortions are common and acceptable on a reasonable level, but not when they are a part of constant negative self-talk.

Let's say you get invited to a party. Your mind perceives that invitation negatively, ignoring the simple fact that you are likable and wanted at the party. Instead, you entertain negative thoughts.

"They invited me out of sympathy, or "I was asked only because I am Alison's friend." "No one will talk to me even if I go!"

Your mind is trying to make you see yourself in an unappreciated negative light under exaggerated and distorted circumstances that are not good or beneficial. But just like constant negative thoughts can be damaging when you allow them to take over your rational thinking patterns, consciously putting a stop to disruptive and self-degrading ideas can help you to overcome your critical analysis of yourself.

Common Types of Cognitive Distortions You May Experience

1. **Dwelling only on the negative**

When your mind filters out all positive reasoning to dwell on the negative—it's called filtering. You forget all the good aspects to focus on that one negativity—which you embrace and feel miserable.

You scored much higher than expected on a challenging exam. Your teacher commends your performance and tells the class about your outstanding achievement. When leaving the class, you are called aside and gently told to try and improve one aspect of the subject to bring your overall grade to an exceptional level. You leave the classroom with your mind dwelling on that one comment about where you must improve, not on the high score you achieved or the praise your teacher publicly gave you but on that one aspect where you were asked to improve. In doing so, your mind has filtered through all positive thoughts to find that one negative emotion to blow out of proportion and focus on creating anxious thoughts.

2. **Overgeneralization or making a mountain out of a molehill**

Such negative cognitive distortions can take place when you over-analyze a general situation.

For example, let's say you make several suggestions at an office brainstorming session. Still, none of them were accepted, and you leave feeling personally scarred, scolding yourself for making such suggestions that made you look mediocre.

Perhaps many others made suggestions that did not get taken up, but your mind blocks them out to focus on your rejection. You even use that negativity to generalize the rest of your situation.

"I will never be good enough for a promotion" and "Nothing good ever works for me."

Can you see how much negative thinking can cause you to suffer unnecessary anxieties?

3. **Personalization of general issues where you voluntarily take the blame**

You voluntarily accept the blame even when you are not directly connected to the incident. The cognitive distortion you are dealing with makes you think it was all your fault, even though there is no way for you to be directly involved.

With this type of distortion, passing the blame on to someone else also occurs. Connecting another person's acts to you makes you think the two are connected and therefore affects the outcome of what happened to you.

- Accepting blame that is not yours—Your child getting hurt at basketball practice could have been avoided if you had only advised them more about being cautious.

- Passing the blame—If your partner had not worked late last night, you could have woken up in time for your important job interview.

4. **Thinking everything is all or nothing—"polarization."**

This cognitive distortion can damage your well-being; your relationships and personality can suffer greatly.

Let's say you are best friends with someone, but suddenly you learn that they spent their weekend having fun with someone else without letting you know first, although you were out of town that weekend and would not have been able to join them.

You would then cut out that person from your life for being "sneaky" and accusing them of hiding their close friendship with someone other than you. It's an all-or-nothing type of negative thinking that can quickly destroy relationships and your self-esteem because, in turn, you go around establishing almost unattainable high standards for yourself.

5. **Jumping to conclusions**

A common trait of overthinking is over-analyzing a situation and then arriving at a negative conclusion even though there is no evidence to support your beliefs. Such thinking causes more damage and anxiety when reacting to that perceived conclusion. Jumping to conclusions can be very disruptive to a relationship.

6. **Not taking responsibility for your actions**

This cognitive distortion makes you think that others are to be blamed for your actions and how you feel. You do not realize that you are, in fact, in complete control of your actions and thoughts. Instead, you go on to believe that outsiders influence your beliefs and behavior. Their distressing actions toward you cause you to

feel sad, disappointed, and angry, resulting in you being unproductive and acting out at work, home, etc.

7. **Becoming predictive of future outcomes and seeing them in a negative light**

You assume and conclude what the future will involve concerning
a specific activity. Your mind perceives the problem, establishes
how it will work in the negative context, and sets the outcome.

"It is no use my applying for the promotion, others are better than
me, and I will not get it because my ideas for the company will be
dismissed. Therefore, I am not going to apply for the promotion!"

You become your judge and jury and give yourself the verdict
leaving you no chance of envisioning a successful outcome for that
event.

8. **Making a massive issue of even minor problems—"catastrophizing."**

You assume the worst of everything. Everything is seen as a cata-
strophe because you keep imagining the worst outcomes. Proper
reasoning goes out the window when you start to assume things
in a negative context.

- What if they decide I am not good enough for the promotion?

- What if the dress I ordered arrives too late for the party?

- What if my car breaks down and I miss my interview?

You deal with many negative thoughts and what-ifs simply because you see the negativity in events above the positivity.

While cognitive distortions can sound disturbing, and you probably identify with some of the examples I have listed here, it is possible to overcome this disruptive overthinking.

Cognitive restructuring is a successful method for dealing with the damages caused by these negative thoughts and can be done by resetting the way you think and perceive a subject. Let me introduce you to some easy techniques that you can adopt.

Cognitive Restructuring—Overcoming Your Cognitive Distortions

Cognitive distortions can be controlled. You can overcome the anxiety and stress damaging overthinking habits are causing you through simple techniques.

Cognitive behavioral therapy (CBT), used to treat anxiety disorders, can help you overcome and reframe your destructive thinking habits through simple techniques that control your thoughts, emotions, and behavior.

Your cognitive distortions influence your thoughts, emotions, and behavior; all three are connected and, in turn, influence each other. Think about it; when you overthink on a dangerous level, your thoughts influence your emotions, and once you are emotionally vulnerable and become uncontrollable, your behavior will match it. For example, overthinking and becoming angry with your partner will automatically make you react and behave in a violent or disruptive way that you will regret later. Therefore, you must learn to stop and get your thoughts, emotions, and behavior under control before you indulge in regrettable or anxious actions.

Identify Your Unique Cognitive Distortion

To begin cognitive restructuring, you must be able to accept and understand your condition. Start by identifying the type of cognitive distortion to which you are vulnerable. Self-monitor and become aware of your thoughts and emotions so you can spot a sudden change in your thinking as the distortion takes over.

Stop giving in to the thought distortion that will manifest as a strong emotion. Tell yourself you are wrong to make assumptions; question your decision and the reasoning behind your thinking.

Question Your Assumptions—Could I be Wrong?

Let's say you are in the habit of overthinking and jumping to conclusions; the first step is to identify that weakness by second guessing your assumptions. Let's say you become overwhelmed with sadness over something you believe your partner meant in one of their statements. Why don't you first analyze that assumption before you think it to be true?

Ask yourself:

- Was what was said meant in that context, or could I be overreacting and assuming what I perceive to be true in my head?

- Did I overreact and assume too much too soon? Could there be no underlying reason for that statement?

Second-guess your assumptions and analyze your sudden conclusion as much as you would a statement or behavior made by someone. Be critical of your assumptions and think that you are not always correct—accept that you could be wrong. Only through second guessing yourself can you begin to take control of your runaway thoughts and decide on a course of action.

Evaluate and Conclude You Were Wrong to Overthink

Let's say you start to second guess your assumptions; you must then go over the evidence to prove to yourself that you were wrong. This is an essential part of the process.

Become objective by evaluating the situation; looking at all angles will help you gauge the situation's good and bad to arrive at a conclusion that may differ from your initial thought.

Let's say you believe you will not get that office promotion you want. By evaluating the pros and cons of the situation, you may find that you are qualified enough and quite eligible to apply for the position, despite your initial reaction of predicting the outcome of your application in a negative light.

As a part of having enough evidence to convince yourself your negative thinking is baseless and inaccurate is to cultivate the habit of making a list of facts that will help you to cancel out those negative thoughts for lack of proper reasoning. In short, you realize that they were wrong and blown out of proportion.

Empathize Your Situation

Do not feed your anxious nature by becoming critical of yourself in an unkind manner. Once you realize that you are susceptible to cognitive distortions, be accepting of your condition and not harsh. In other words, become sympathetic about your situation but not to an extent where you create anxiety, just enough for you to avoid negatively putting yourself down for having a weakness. Think of your discovery as a step in the right direction to finding a solution and finally healing yourself to be free of the damaging effects that overthinking can cause.

Once you become more critical of your thoughts and emotions, you can control your behavior better. Learn to shift your ideas and change the direction you are going because you suddenly recognize the destructive path on which you are treading. It is not easy to change habits or a pattern of thinking you have cultivated over the years, but through a conscious effort, you can.

Avoid the triggers. Do not put too much stress on yourself; stop setting the bar too high. Do not set yourself a schedule of "must-do" tasks. Instead, take it slow and do what is within your limits. I am not asking you to settle, but I am asking you to try and see the gravity of trying to meet your high expectations all the time—it is a gradual build of stress that eventually leads to negative self-talk and anxiety.

Work on Cognitive Restructuring as a Do-it-Yourself Recovery Technique and Reap the Benefits

You can learn the techniques to overcome your cognitive distortions without the help of a therapist. However, professional help will initially guide getting started and show the path. In the meantime, knowing how the techniques work will be highly beneficial for self-healing and enjoying the following for your overall well-being.

- You can learn to overcome anxiety on your own by controlling your thoughts, emotions, and behavior by simply being aware.

- Establish stronger bonds and lasting relationships by being more open and maintaining healthy relationships instead of those rife with overthinking-induced suspicions, guilt, and disappointments.

- Strengthen your self-esteem, become more aware of your capabilities, and stop being unkindly critical of yourself.

- Stop the habit of resorting to coping mechanisms damaging your overall health—seeking comfort in food and overeating, substance abuse, and treating yourself with little respect.

Look Forward to Enjoying Life Through Simple Changes to Your Thoughts, Emotions, and Behavior

There are several benefits to cognitive restructuring; you can go on to enjoy healthier relationships and a brighter outlook on life—more importantly, you can begin to let go of your anxieties.

The practice of mindfully restructuring your cognitive behavior can help with the following:

- Dealing with eating disorders—obesity, bulimia, and anorexia

- Help mend relationship problems

- PTSD

- Mental disorders

Here are some tips for reaping the most benefits of overcoming cognitive distortions. These proven practices are helpful and healthy habits to cultivate as they lead to a happier and more fulfilling lifestyle. Try and adopt these habits by being strong, avoiding negative thoughts from invading your mind, and choosing to embrace positive vibes as your first thought each day.

1. **Begin your day happy and on a positive note**

Direct your mind toward positive thoughts. When you wake up, practice a self-reflective exercise where you choose to be optimistic and happy. Become conscious of the warmth of the sunlight on your face. Sunlight influences the secretion of a hormone called serotonin which is responsible for making you feel good, alert, and in a better mood to face the day. Embrace the potential the new day holds. Let go of your inhibitions; they belong in the past. You can look forward to starting with a clean sheet each day.

Tips to Start Your Day on a Positive Vibe

- Wake up early—don't choose to lie in bed and then start your day in a rush. Get used to waking up early, so you have time to savor the day. Enjoy a morning beverage outside, watch the sunrise, and plan your day.

- Meditate—a brief 30-minute mindfulness meditation session to prepare yourself mentally to face the day with a positive vibe will help you clarify your thoughts and focus on your daily tasks.

- Deep breathing exercises are just as effective as meditation and help you to gain focus while improving your concentration power. Learn to take control of your mind and prevent little negative thoughts from invading your mind all the time. They are toxic and cause a lot of disruptions, especially with your relationships.

- Go for a jog and enjoy the feeling as your heart starts pumping, raising your metabolism and zest, thus, energizing you to face the day. Jogging also encourages the release of serotonin, your feel-good hormone, and endorphins. Endorphins are chemicals released by your body as a stress reliever and are neurotransmitters secreted to help you deal with stress. Therefore, running and jogging are stressbusters and highly beneficial exercises for relieving anxiety and depression (Anderson & Shivakumar, 2013).

- Exercise and establish a routine. Start a morning fitness program that works for you. It can be any type of physical activity you like. Aerobics, swimming, dancing, cycling, etcetera.

- Start journaling. Maintain a focus journal, and you can create an outlet to transfer your anxieties out of your mind. Journaling also helps you to take a more in-depth view of your thoughts to analyze and see your worries from a different perspective. Your sadness toward something your partner said may not seem so bleak when you write it out. You may even realize you overreacted and your initial understanding and deduction of what your partner said were wrong. Journaling can also help you establish an affirmation for the day—a goal to follow; "I will not let random thoughts invade my mind." Get started with the journaling prompts and worksheets provided in chapter 10.

2. **Focus on positive thoughts**

An optimistic person will have more positive thoughts running through their mind, while a pessimist will be burdened by negative issues, which is what we are trying to avoid. There is research to back up these claims. Studies have confirmed that GAD, which deals with pathological worry, is significantly reduced through positive thought replacement (Eagleson, 2016).

To focus on positive thinking is not to live in a fantasy land and ignore everything around you; to focus on positive thoughts is to accept life's trials more enthusiastically—the glass is half-full approach.

You cannot stop the endless stream of thoughts that passes through your mind, but you can control how much importance you give those thoughts. If you embrace the negativity, you open your-self up for cognitive distortions, anxiety, and stress triggers. Your thoughts will naturally dwell more on the negative, but through conscious efforts, you can shift your thinking, which is what you will be doing when you practice positive thinking.

How Can I Encourage Positive Thinking?

It is much simpler than you think and certainly kinder and more effortless than dealing with negativity and the disturbing emotions it influences. Make a resolve to initiate new habits, to change your negative thoughts into positive vibes using these simple tips and an open attitude to go beyond what is familiar to you.

- Keep a tab on your thoughts. You know how sneaky those negative thoughts that creep into your mind can be; one minute, you are fine, and the next, you are overthinking the possibility of a different outcome had you handled a past event differently.

- Make a list of your ambitions to change. Once you start making a conscious effort to keep a tab of your thoughts, you will notice the triggers, and areas you tend to over-think. Perhaps it is related to your work, relationship, or general attitude where you second guess your decisions. Make a list of the areas you are prone to negative thoughts and try to change your thinking and the usual angle you take by looking for positive options or reasons instead.

- Discover self-worth. Your negative thoughts of yourself cause the most damage. Likewise, you hold the power to uplift yourself as well. Daily affirmations where you give yourself a little positive pep talk will help you to change your low self-esteem to discover you are much stronger and more special than you give yourself credit.

- Here are three powerful daily affirmations you can use to expand on and teach yourself to be thankful for who you are.

- I am much stronger than I believe myself to be.

- I am complete. All I need is within myself.

- I am focused and confident to face the day.

- Learn to let go and take it easy. Smile and laugh even in your bleakest moments, and you will feel less stressed. Humor has a magical power to alleviate the darkest of moods if you allow it. Quite often, we are more comfortable accepting unhappiness than seeing the humor in moments of despair simply because we feel it is the more appropriate emotion.

The benefits of humor on mental health are invaluable; humor can trigger feel-good emotions and induce positive short-term changes in a person's mental health status (Berger et al., 2021).

3. Choose to hang around with people with a positive outlook on life.

Avoid negative influences and toxic people. Instead, make sure the people you associate with are those that uplift your mood and encourage you to be positive and reach your highest potential. People who support you will keep you alert to your anxieties and help you diffuse your worries, while people who negatively influence you will add to your self-doubts and anxiety.

How Positive Thinking Can Help Your Relationships

A relationship thrives on the amount of effort you put into maintaining that bond. Focusing on a relationship's positive aspects is crucial for continuing a healthy relationship. Focusing on the negative factors of your relationship will only highlight the things you dislike and hide all the positive elements.

It is easy to pay attention to faults and what you want to change in your relationship rather than see how much love, devotion, compassion, and warmth you take for granted while unconsciously enjoying those privileges.

Having an honest and open bond with someone is to be treasured and seen in a positive light. Therefore, use positive thinking to show yourself the value of your relationship; consciously avoid high expectations or comparing your relationship status with what others have. We are all different from each other, and the combination that two people create is unique. You cannot liken it to what other people have. Therefore, comparisons and expectations based on generalized relationship features must be avoided.

Use Positive Thinking to Cultivate Healthy Relationships

Relationships are not limited to romance; maintaining friendships and close contact with people you feel a link to is vital for support, enjoying companionship, and a sense of belonging.

If you are prone to overthinking and cognitive distortions, you may be distancing yourself from people and limiting your interactions. Isolation is one of the key triggers for aggravating anxiety disorders and has been linked to health disorders that include insomnia and other sleep disorders, as well as problems with the immune system. Conversely, anxiety, low self-esteem, and depression can encourage social isolation; therefore, it's essential to use positive thinking to avoid falling into the bracket of loneliness.

Stress and anxiety, which increases due to social isolation, can cause problems with your immune system when the stress hormone cortisol is released. Cortisol levels, when increased, reduce the number of white blood cells (lymphocytes) essential to keep your immune system on alert and ready to hunt for bacteria and fight infections making you more vulnerable to infections. However, this is just one reason for you to start using positive thinking to improve your interactions and relationships with others. Let's look at it more.

1. **Improve your interpersonal relationships**

Improve your interpersonal relationships by first accepting yourself. Using the power of positivity to build self-worth will, in turn, help you to realize that you are worthy of maintaining healthy relationships with others and there is no necessity to choose isolation. Accepting yourself will help you to accept others and build healthy relationships free from the stress of overthinking about your worthiness to be a part of a healthy community of friends.

2. **Use Positivity to Maintain Your Relationships**

Romantic or otherwise, relationships need to be maintained. Being an overthinker will not work if you are prone to cognitive distortions where you overanalyze problems within your relationships. Using positive thinking to keep your irrational thoughts at bay will stop you from sabotaging a good relationship.

3. **Use Positivity to Be More Understanding**

Look at the bigger picture and be more open to problems rather than being quick to judge and dismiss a good relationship. You may be able to identify with sabotaging several good relationships you would have enjoyed in the past. No matter how good and positive those relationships were, you would have chosen to abandon them the moment a problem cropped up that hurt your feelings. Use positive thinking to look at the bigger picture, question the reasons behind the problem, and choose to be critical of your conclusions. Journaling is an excellent method to take apart your initial reactions and look at them from a different perspective to your initial response.

4. **Increase Your Popularity Through Positivity**

Being around someone who is easily upset and moody can be an exhausting experience, even for the most cheerful people. While you are not required to suddenly change your stance to someone with a permanently sunny disposition, you may find a huge benefit in uplifting your mood by being more positive.

Positive thinking can change your general attitude to a more re-laxed and easy-going composure. It will, in turn, make you a more approachable person—let's not forget the lowered levels of stress you will enjoy by keeping your thoughts positive.

Cultivating a more optimistic approach to your life's challenges and becoming more determined to achieve your goals will help you to manifest them better by not feeding your stress, panic, and natural tendency to be anxious all the time. Try to let go of and cancel out your anxieties by evaluating your negative emotions every time you overthink—ask yourself, "why am I feeling this way? Did I assess the situation correctly?"

Staying focused on your end goal, the inner peace, and the lifestyle change you envision at the end of your transformative journey is your motivational factors. Let's begin the journey by identifying your triggers. Stop the negativity and anxiety before it starts.

CHAPTER 4

— • —

KNOW YOUR TRIGGERS

I know you think I'm overreacting about the silliest little things, but to me those silly little things seem like the doom the world could bring. —Tiffaney L Ganci (Ganci, 2018)

Anxiety can engulf you in one sudden bout of panic, or it can build up over time as stress. Either way, you may already know the cues for when your negative thoughts are starting to grow, making you overwhelmed, scared and trapped. What if you could find a button that simply says "stop"?

Identifying your negative triggers is your stop button. In this chapter, I will help you find them, look at methods for dealing with your fears and weaknesses, and at techniques to overcome future anxiety or panic attacks by controlling your thoughts, emotions, and behavior.

You Are Not Alone, Stay Motivated and Overcome Your Anxieties—Ariana Grande is Your Inspiration!

Ariana Grande may be wildly successful and famous, but she is also a person dealing with anxiety and makes no effort to hide the fact. As a mental health advocate, her message to others coping with anxiety and depression-related conditions is to end the stigma and reach out for help. Ariana has made no effort to hide her anxiety and the stress she deals with, stating that the road to recovery is neither straightforward nor fun but one that you must travel based on commitment and a strong will to recover. Admitting to dealing with PTSD due to the 2017 terrorist attack at her concert in Manchester, England, this star is determined to heal and inspire others to follow her path by staying true to themselves and realizing their self-worth (Gomez, 2019).

One of the most successful tools for dealing with your anxiety triggers is acceptance; acknowledging your condition and the need for help is how you set yourself in the right direction facing the path to recovery. Ariana Grande is on that path. Are you ready to follow her?

What Are Anxiety Triggers?

Your profound emotional reaction toward an event, incident, conversation, or anything else emotionally disturbing, is what it means to be triggered by anxiety. Remembering past traumatic events can cause distressing reactions, making those agonizing memories emotional triggers.

We all experience discomfort brought on by remembering an incident, something we said or did, or an uncomfortable situation we had to face in the past that was embarrassing or even upsetting. Although unpleasant, these memories do not incite profound, disruptive, and disturbing mental reactions if you are not dealing with a mental health disorder. Those that do are classified as emotional triggers and will profoundly affect people with anxiety conditions.

Emotional triggers can damage your mental state and may lead to trauma that can cause lasting damage—when left untreated. Someone experiencing a traumatic emotional trigger blanks out, loses focus, and zones out of the present situation. Their minds may get transported back to the traumatic event that caused the emotional trigger to develop. They become trapped in their fear, unable to break free, and realize they are not in the dangerous situation the trigger has created in their mind.

An emotional trigger can be something that develops through a sudden traumatic event or a long-term emotionally abusive situation or trauma. It can be an external factor, such as seeing someone who resembles an abusive partner, a smell, a word, a particular phrase associated with the trauma, or a sound that triggers a memory.

A trigger can be internal, like a sudden thought that springs to your mind prompting an avalanche of memories and emotions. Even the feeling of deja vu can turn into an emotional trigger because of the traumatic memory it could incite.

People with PTSD are most vulnerable to triggers caused by external factors such as images or hearing about an event like the one that caused PTSD to develop. For example, being a victim of a terrorist attack may make you nervous about sudden sounds or being in crowds. That is one of the reasons trigger warnings are given at the beginning of content containing common emotional triggers—violent scenes, blood, bombings, etc. Recent studies, however, dispute the practicality of trigger warnings which we will discuss later in this chapter.

Categorizing Triggers

As I mentioned, there are two types of triggers: internal and external. An emotion causes internal triggers, a sudden sensation you may experience physically that triggers a memory. Extreme sweating, a raised heart rate, feeling tense, restless, nervous, angry, or feelings of dread are some of the physical sensations you may feel that link your emotion to a past event.

External triggers can be anything; a common incident that seems quite normal for most people but traumatic if you are dealing with anxiety. External triggers are often linked to a past occurrence. A television show that deals with domestic violence could cause emotional triggers in someone who must deal with a violent spouse. An argument that dredges up memories of traumatic times could turn into an emotional trigger and lead to anxiety where the person loses control of the present situation and becomes trapped in a moment from the past because their minds have suddenly rebooted and are living in that traumatic incident once more.

Emotional triggers are not always linked to a particular emotion; they can manifest from feelings of sadness, fear, disappointment, anger, and loneliness. Social anxieties and panic disorders are often the type of mental health conditions strongly associated with triggers.

What are the Most Common and Often Un-Thought of Factors That Cause Triggers?

Understanding the reason behind a trigger will give you more power to conquer that trigger. Also, despite it being a common practice to include trigger warnings for just about everything, anxiety triggers are not always based on sensitive issues. A person dealing with anxiety triggers is not always an emotionally weak and overly sensitive individual—that perception is wrong.

An emotional trigger can be based on fears that are a part of someone's reality or words that can cause deep wounds mentally—wounds that are still sore and not healing. Emotional triggers are reminders of the horrors that someone went through, emotional scarring that needs a chance to heal. Being affected by a specific stimulus makes you vulnerable to anxieties that can be triggered by prevalent factors we often take for granted.

Did you know that caffeine can be an emotional trigger for some people?

It can be, especially since caffeine has the power to influence your central nervous system.

Most of us love caffeine because of its ability to stimulate our energy levels by upping our metabolism to make us alert, active, and ready to face the day with zest. However, think twice about overindulging in caffeine because too much of a good thing can cause you harm. A side effect of too much caffeine can cause you to become nervous and even anxious if you aren't dealing with a mental health disorder. The biggest culprits are coffee which contains high levels of caffeine, and energy drinks.

Thyroid Diseases can Affect Your Mood and Cause Anxiety.

The thyroid is a gland in your neck, a part of your endocrine system—the network of glands that secrete hormones. The thyroid secretes hormones that affect the function of your body, mainly thyroxine (T4) and triiodothyronine (T3) which influence your metabolism and the energy needed for your food to digest. Thyroid hormones are suspected of influencing the levels of the mood hormone serotonin secreted from your brain and are therefore, a possible link to anxiety and depression for some people (Bauer et al., 2002).

- Hyperthyroidism is a condition that occurs when your thyroid gland is overactive. Heightened anxiety, restlessness, and over irritability are often the symptoms.

- On the other hand, hypothyroidism is an underactive thyroid gland linked to depression with symptoms of heightened fatigue.

Anxiety and depression are not the only symptoms of thyroid diseases. Several physical symptoms (a change in your heart rate, hair loss, sudden weight gain, etc.) indicate a gland problem. Your healthcare provider will evaluate you for symptoms before asking you to take a test to check the function of your thyroid gland and then narrow the results for a possible link to your anxiety.

Alcohol Can Be Less Relaxing and More of an Anxiety Trigger

Alcohol, when imbibed in excess, can have the opposite effect of the perceived calming and relaxing qualities a glass of wine is thought to offer. Alcohol affects people with anxiety badly and may aggravate their symptoms. Also, alcohol or substance abuse is higher among people with mental health issues (National Institute on Drug Abuse, 2020).

Neglect of Oneself and Missing Out on Basic Self-Care Can Trigger Depression

Do you often find yourself in your pajamas at midday, hair unbrushed, and skipping regular baths? These are signs that you may be dealing with depression or anxiety. Conversely, cultivating this behavior can lead to anxiety, making it a trigger. Not taking care of yourself and having inadequate hygiene often lead to low self-esteem, one of the triggers of anxiety disorders. It is essential to take care of your basic needs, be well groomed, and ensure your physical and mental needs are met healthily, contributing to your overall well-being. Therefore, neglecting oneself is a trait that takes away enthusiasm and can conversely indicate an individual dealing with depression.

A Lack of Proper Sleep Can Make You Anxious

The amount of stress put on the importance of a good night's sleep is substantiated by research that clearly shows we need proper rest for our body and mind to recalibrate thoughts, rejuvenate and heal—and nothing beats a good night's sleep. The occasional all-nighter is not going to cause harm. Still, if you make it a regular habit to stay up all night, you will eventually experience mental and physical changes. Cognitive changes could reflect stress and anxiety caused by a lack of sleep.

Trauma When Experienced on a Personal Level Can Become a Mental Trigger

Trauma makes you vulnerable, and your physical and emotional self feels threatened. Commonly the fight or flight reaction associated with anxiety is high when dealing with a particular incident or event causing your trauma—PTSD is a common condition related to trauma.

Trauma can set off a nervous disposition in you, making you sensitive to what you think are common everyday activities—being in a crowded place or even hanging out with friends. That nervous disposition makes your usual composure feel threatened when planning for these events, causing stress to build up—and unnoticed to you, the nervousness that ensues is a trigger increasing your anxiety.

Social Anxiety and Stress Triggers

Dealing with social anxiety can make social gatherings a trigger. It could be a simple get-together of friends or even meeting family—the anxiety will be genuine and cause you to become nervous and anxious at the thought of the upcoming event.

Your Messy Home Could Be a Trigger for Your Anxiety

Dealing with anxiety-related conditions can make seemingly mundane situations much more stressful than usual. A messy home is one. Someone dealing with anxiety will find the clutter in their home unbearable and cleaning up will prioritize their schedule of things to get done. If that is the case, and you are too busy to get down to cleaning, the sight and thought of the clutter will keep making you more and more anxious on a subconscious level as you do your daily work. That nagging thought of a cluttered home will remain at the back of your mind like a trigger causing you to become more stressed.

Dealing With Your Finances is a Trigger for Anxiety

Your finances can be a trigger whether you are on a shoestring budget or enjoying a comfortable lifestyle. Your anxieties can make it seem like a huge burden to keep track of and maintain your expenses and income. Overthinking about your finances will act as a trigger to cause you panic, stress, and anxiety. Just like cleaning your home will eliminate the trigger, you can reduce the amount of pressure you face with your monetary issues by constructing a plan. Draw up a financial plan that will help you to identify your expenses and income and keep track of changes, thus avoiding the stress of worrying about budgets, expenses, and balances.

Your Relationships Can Become Stressful

Tension, a difference of opinion, and pressure can make relationships with the people you love an anxiety trigger. Despite loving those closest to you, there are times you cannot avoid the different opinions or pressure put on you by partners, children, or parents. Incidents, events, or situations dealing with family that cause you to become anxious are triggers. Tension is one of the biggest culprits. When left unresolved or ignored, as is often the case in a family unit, it can build up and explode into an unpleasant episode of anger, resentment, and frustration. If you are dealing with an anxiety disorder, such triggers can become unbearable, especially when linked to people you care about are concerned.

Conflict is Unpleasant and Hard to Deal with as an Anxiety Trigger

A person dealing with anxiety will find conflict a hard-to-handle trigger that ignites their nervous disposition. Arguments in the workplace, with your partner, or with family members are all triggers that instigate the fight or flight reaction in you. Conflict can affect you when you are confused and overwhelmed. Even a disagreement online may set off your anxieties because you don't know how to deal with the emotions. Learning to manage your reaction to a conflict will be just as effective as having a plan for your finances. Teaching yourself not to panic and to approach conflict calmly is a skill that will take time, but through conscious effort, it is attainable. It's a simple case of mind over matter.

Triggers That Are Linked to General Events

Events, situations, and reasons that make us unhappy, angry, and frustrated can be more serious than you would give them credit. They could be responsible for your stress levels increasing as a trigger for the development of anxiety syndromes. It all depends on how you deal with these everyday stresses; divorce, children leaving home, a death, the end of a relationship, and other events that can ignite emotional distress and pain are often ignored or not acknowledged. However, the pain and anguish, when not dealt with, will remain, triggered by events or situations that refresh the hurt over and over until you develop an anxiety disorder. Ignoring a hurtful situation will not make it disappear, nor will getting busy and choosing to avoid thinking about a distressing problem for you. Acknowledging and accepting pain is the best method to prevent that pain from turning into a trigger that will affect your well-being and quality of life. Triggers must be faced. Avoiding them and running away from anxiety-causing situations prevent you from reaching a solution, and you must live with those provocations—choose to be free!

You Cannot Outrun or Hide from Your Triggers

Stop avoiding your triggers. It is causing you more harm than you know!

More and more mental health experts and researchers are questioning the benefit of advising people with anxiety issues to avoid their triggers—with more leaning toward the practice being harmful.

Avoiding situations, people, and places that make us uncomfortable or seem harmful is an instinct and is another fail-safe mechanism linked to anxiety traits that help keep us safe—when it is within the natural parameters.

When dealing with anxiety, avoiding triggers becomes essential; you try to prevent your panic attacks and anxiety from happening by staying away from potential triggers. Plus, there is plenty of support, too, where trigger warnings are issued to help you decide about becoming exposed to a possible stimulus. But how long can you keep avoiding triggers and dealing with the problems connected to your avoidance behavior? For example, if you are dealing with social anxiety, how long can you avoid going out for public events or socializing before your relationships and friendships start to suffer?

Is it Healthy to Avoid Triggers?

During the process of avoiding triggers, you are also avoiding experiences that will help you overcome your anxieties and grow stronger. You are avoiding a significant portion of encounters that will shape and teach you to cope with life's unexpected twists and turns, which are necessary trials to help you overcome your fears, and doubts avoiding a lack of self-confidence.

When you avoid your anxiety triggers,

- Are you not telling yourself you are weak and incapable of facing and dealing with your fears?

- How will you learn to cope with and get over your anxieties?

- How much are you willing to sacrifice to avoid your triggers?

Taking the trouble to avoid your fears is a successful method of maintaining your anxieties and triggers!

The New Reasoning Surrounding the Avoidance of Anxiety Triggers

There are many reasons for experts to advise against the new culture of avoiding anxiety triggers. Let's start with the obvious.

1. It's nearly Impossible to Avoid Triggers All the Time

Unless you live in a bubble, how long can you keep avoiding your emotional triggers and attempt to live a normal life? It's nearly impossible.

Let's say you are watching the evening news on the television and a trigger warning comes up. Do you run away to the next room or ask that the television be turned off so that ultimately no one in your family knows what the news is?

Do you never go out for a party, a concert, or a social gathering with your partner because you are dealing with a social phobia? Are you willing to test the limits of your relationship to avoid the triggers, or will you try to conquer your fears and move away from your anxieties while moving your life along?

Facing your fears is all about dealing with anxieties, and avoidance certainly is not a healthy option. Emotional triggers can take place anywhere at any time, making them nearly impossible to avoid; the solution is to find ways to cope by exposing yourself to your fears—it's easier to fight a known enemy than deal with uncertainty.

2. **Avoidance Behavior Leads to Missing Out on More Than Just Your Fears**

You avoid your company's New Years' Eve Party because you fear intimacy, too many hugs, and wishes for a happy season. So, you stay at home alone while everyone you know attends the party; the next day, you go to work and ask to see the pictures, and they are amazing, showing you what a fabulous party you missed. Not only did you avoid triggering your social phobias, but you avoided spending New Year's Eve with your friends, enjoying a feeling of belonging and togetherness—instead of the loneliness you felt spending the evening at home.

Avoidance behavior can be a real bummer and disappointment because you miss out on so many life experiences that would ultimately help you with your anxieties. You miss out on more treats that avoid your emotional triggers. You miss experiencing places, friendships, and being in a close relationship because you constantly try to prevent an emotional trigger. Still, chances are those emotional triggers will crop up at some time while some fabulous experiences you miss cannot be replaced.

3. **The Longer and More You Avoid Triggers, the Worse They Get**

Your goal is to heal your anxieties and not safeguard them; avoiding triggers will only cause them to grow and thrive. Your pain will remain fresh and untreated as long as you avoid trying to heal. You become more sensitive to your fears because you have no exposure to them. Your emotional triggers and fears keep growing until you become a slave to them, seeking ways to avoid and hide from anything and everyone you fear will cause you anxiety. You barely realize you have created a whole new anxiety for yourself; the anxiety and stress of avoidance and deprivation of life experiences.

4. **How Can You Identify and Question Your Cognitive Distortions When You Avoid Triggers?**

Overthinking and cognitive distortions take place when your anxieties are triggered. In the previous chapter, we learned about substituting positive thoughts for negative and practicing cognitive restructuring to avoid damaging behavior that sabotages your relationships and negatively impacts so much more of your lifestyle.

The critical element of "fixing" your cognitive distortions is recognition, to become aware of your distortive thinking habits. Those distortions occur through heightened emotions like sadness, anger, disappointment, and other emotions that wreak havoc with your thinking and process of reasoning.

But what if you avoid situations where those emotions are triggered? Does that mean your cognitive distortions go away? It does not.

Avoidance is not the solution. The solution comes from being aware and choosing to change consciously. Avoidance and awareness cannot work together. Avoidance is a negative trait, while awareness and coping are positive methods of dealing with anxiety.

Let's look for positive solutions for dealing with anxiety and triggers.

Managing and Dealing with Your Anxiety Triggers

Start by acknowledging your anxiety and the triggers. They are very real stresses and are not to be stigmatized. You are not alone when dealing with your mental health condition because you are in a situation that millions across the world face—now it's time you choose to heal through awareness.

Before you formulate a plan, it's essential to identify your triggers positively; become attuned to your moods and when they change. Experiment and be aware of what and who causes your anxieties to increase or *where* your mood alterations take place. Make a note of them. Use your focus journal to log your thoughts and discoveries; work through them to make proper conclusions. List your findings and be honest with yourself. Practice confidence and choose the emotional triggers you strongly believe you can get under control.

Develop a better understanding of the triggers you face regularly. Keep in mind that avoidance of any triggers is not an option. What you are trying to do is limit how much hold a trigger has on you.

Aim to manage and deal with your anxieties starting at a basic level. Once your confidence grows, and your fear of your emotional triggers reduces, you will become stronger and find better ways to block those triggers from affecting you rather than avoiding them as a short-term and somewhat erratic solution.

The techniques I suggest here are for you to develop healthy habits starting with your mind and body. They are simple changes that will make you more focused and better equipped mentally and physically to face challenges. Dealing with mental health conditions is not limited to healing your mind. Your physical self must be healthy and robust to assist your mind.

You will notice that strengthening your mind and body is as simple as avoiding certain habits and cultivating others that will instill self-confidence and a sense of achievement—the ultimate goal is to realize that *you* control your thoughts, emotions, and behavior.

Coping and Dealing with Anxiety Triggers—The Best Methods

1. Practice Controlling Your Emotions

Learn to regulate your emotions and keep them in check.

It is normal to experience different emotions from time to time due to circumstances or situations. Feeling sad when your children finally leave home or getting irritated with a slow-moving cash teller at the bank are some examples where you experience a heightened emotion and then get it in check. Emotional regulation is almost automatic as you react to situations and circumstances.

When there is no emotional regulation, you feel increased lows and highs beyond the normal range. And it is not healthy. Those extreme emotional fluctuations are what lead to triggers causing you to panic.

You can go from relaxed to dealing with uncontrollable rage in minutes through sudden triggers. Your relationships suffer, and you become unpredictable to yourself and others in your circle.

The good news is you can learn to get your emotions in check by learning emotional regulation. You must know people who exert extreme restraint when it comes to keeping their emotions under control. They exhibit what is called high emotional intelligence.

Such people have good coping mechanisms, although they experience negative emotions like everyone else. They are skilled in emotional self-regulation, which you can learn through practice.

Tips to Manifest Emotional Self-Regulation

Identify and stop—whenever you feel a strong emotion overtaking your thoughts and behavior, make a conscious effort to stop. Pause instead of encouraging the emotional trigger; practice a few deep breaths and see what you feel next. Chances are the heightened emotion is going to deflate somewhat during your pause. It's not easy to switch from a volatile nature to exhibiting calm and restraint—but it can be done through determination and practicing the tips I am listing next.

- **Become your own therapist**

This is the most fun part of experiencing a strong emotion. Once you pause the emotional trigger, step in to evaluate the feeling. If you are feeling outraged, ask yourself from where the trigger is manifesting itself. Is it a deep burning sensation in your chest sending out waves of anger? Are your cheeks flushed, and can you almost hear your heart beating way too fast? Getting busy identifying the changes that are taking place in you physically will diffuse the severity of that emotion, making your response to it milder.

- **Try to identify**

Quite often, heightened emotions come in packages. For example, anger may ride in waves of frustration, disappointment, and fear. You may not identify those emotions at first and focus on the rage.

But give the emotion a second analysis, and you will discover the other emotions behind what you are feeling. Quite often, fear is a trigger that sets off those other emotions.

For example, the fear of being perceived as weak will often lead to aggressiveness and anger because you don't want to be viewed as someone vulnerable. In truth, you probably are still vulnerable, maybe due to past trauma, an incident of being bullied when you were younger instigated the need not to look weak as an adult. Therefore, your trigger is the threat of being exposed—you cover up your vulnerability by distracting the attention toward that fact with anger.

Diffuse falling victim to that trigger by accepting your emotion. If you fear vulnerability accept the emotion and who you are—someone who is sensitive and easily hurt. Once you accept the sentiment, in this case, vulnerability, you no longer fear being found out, and therefore there is no trigger for anger to take over! Do you see how the chain reaction works?

- **Practice positive self-talk**

Do not easily give in to your highs and lows; when your sudden and uncontrollable emotional outbursts are making you extremely unhappy—stop and take charge so that they are no longer "uncontrollable." Chances are your volatile behavior will have you berating yourself over and over.

Losing control and yelling at your partner, which results in them leaving, will soon have you switching from a heightened state of anger to a lowered state of despair and depression.

Negative and conflicting thoughts will abound after an outburst.

I drove him away once more, but he can be so unreasonable.

It's all my fault, and I can't control myself.

These negative thoughts will be tumbling around your mind making you feel inferior and a failure when you are not! Be kinder to yourself and, at the same time, be reasonable. What you can do instead of talking down to yourself is to add some positivity to your mind—and use reasoning to come to a solution.

He tries hard to understand me. I should not overreact so much.

I could be wrong to assume they are being unreasonable all the time.

A bit of positivity and reasoning will help you to change your perspective and realize your overactive emotion is clouding your judgment.

- **Take control of your reactions**

When you know that you are overly emotional, and your responses are often aggressive and overwhelming for most people interacting with you—stop before you respond.

If you suddenly feel excited about what someone is saying and want to respond angrily, aggressively, and assertively, check yourself and hold back. Your response is optional every time. Letting comments slide on and off is quite alright.

How many times have you responded aggressively and then regretted it when you saw the reaction in others? You may have noticed how some people tend to keep away from you or are not as "chatty" around you. Your partner may be cautious of how they interact with you. These are all reactions to your explosive nature. If it is making you unhappy then change. Hold back your responses. Count to ten before you respond, and chances are you will not feel so passionate about your reaction.

2. Take Control of Your Life

Aimlessly going about with no plan of your needs, daily interactions, finances, children's schedules, and household needs will only result in you becoming overwhelmed and suffocating under pressure.

Have a to-do list of essential errands you need to run for the day and another for tasks that can be completed in between but are flexible. That way, you don't overwhelm yourself with a long to-do list.

You can do your finances or exam preparations according to a focus plan. One that will help you to have control over your life and the factors that trigger your anxieties. Planning can be very beneficial for managing your stress and triggers.

Avoid falling into depression and dealing with low self-esteem by having goal-oriented methodologies to keep you on track, so you know just where you are heading in life. Plans will help you to become self-aware. When you plan, you will evaluate your capabilities, needs, and strengths; you can learn to avoid suddenly being depressed and anxious about your life's path.

3. **Establish Healthy Boundaries**

Sometimes you must stay away from certain people or say "no" to requests or situations. Exercise that right and avoid stretching yourself to the limit and then enduring a panic attack that sets back your anxiety.

Surround yourself with supportive friends and family. If you fear a relationship or friendship is one-sided, distance yourself from the situation, and you will find you can make better connections later.

Establish limits and boundaries if your job or family life is too demanding. You are not required to work past your office hours if you have other commitments centered on taking care of your needs—those are important.

Teach your partner and children to be independent instead of pandering to their needs and taxing your limits so that you end up burned out and dealing with a meltdown. Establishing healthy boundaries in all aspects of your life will give you more self-worth. You will also manage your time better and enjoy more "me" time.

Another critical boundary you should establish is how long you spend on social media. Avoid comparing yourself to the fictional lives portrayed on popular social media platforms. Did you know several popular influencers have admitted to dealing with anxiety-related conditions? What others display publicly has no bearing on your achievements or life. Avoid comparisons and the negative thoughts that follow.

4. Don't Endure the Journey Alone

Avoid one of the most significant triggers of anxiety—isolation. Choose to be a part of a community and avoid feeling alone. Even if you do not have a family, there are several ways to go out and make friends. Give back to your community by volunteering at shelters. Join a support group by searching for those listed online and close to your home; get used to sharing your worries with others you know are sympathetic and understanding.

Stay within your comfort zone and share what you want; I am not asking you to reveal details about your life you wish to keep private. Instead, share the stories and experiences you can discuss so you don't carry the burden yourself. Sometimes hearing yourself talk puts a whole new perspective on a feeling or thought.

Don't feel shy or awkward asking for and accepting help when available and offered. One good example is postpartum depression which inflicts many new mothers. You can avoid most of the stress and anxiety of caring for a new baby by asking for support. Do not expect to be a supermom and handle it all alone. A spouse, family member, friend, or even a hired helper can ease the burden by pitching in, helping with housework, and taking care of the baby so you don't end up overwhelmed and neglecting yourself.

5. **Practice Meditation or Yoga as Non-Pharmacological Remedies**

Self-reflection will help you to understand your anxieties and triggers better. Yoga and meditation are good non-pharmacological remedies (medication free) for managing anxiety.

Yoga and meditation help form a connection between your mind and body. Through yoga, you develop self-awareness. Research reveals yoga can reduce stress hormones by increasing feel-good neurotransmitters in your brain, thus reducing anxiety and depression (Azami et al., 2018). The practice also encourages clean eating and healthy habits.

Mindfulness meditation is another remedy that helps you to focus. The practice teaches you to be in the moment by becoming aware of what you are doing then, thus, preventing your mind from wandering and focusing on negativities. Mindfulness meditation works in comparison with deep breathing.

Let's say you are sitting in at an office meeting; do so minus the agenda that would typically be running through your mind—your to-do list, what to cook for dinner, your project deadline, etc. Through mindfulness, be present in body and mind at the meeting. Listen, observe, and become aware of your surroundings and what is said.

6. **Consult a Professional Therapist**

A qualified therapist can help you resolve your anxieties and fears, face them, and better understand your triggers. A therapist is qualified to guide you and help you find solutions through self-reflection and analysis. They are also ideal for having a sympathetic ear to unburden and work on a solution through gentle guidance.

A therapist is ideal as a last resort for dealing with triggers you find challenging to get under control. When you find your anxieties are too much to deal with on your own, or when your triggers and worries start to impact your work, relationships, and overall lifestyle, it's time to seek professional help. Speak to your health-care provider about the best type of mental health care professional to consult.

Therapeutic Options for Coping with Triggers That Won't Go Away

As there are several types of anxiety disorders, therapy too should be streamlined to meet those needs. Counseling is a fundamental and short-term therapeutic help that helps you figure out methods to manage your anxieties through discussions. Discussions can work through a group with people experiencing similar symptoms and problems or as a one-on-one session with a qualified counselor. Counseling works on the surface and will not go too deep to explore anxieties; therefore, it is advisable to seek more comprehensive therapeutic help for deep-seated anxieties and triggers.

Exposure Therapy

I would start with this type of therapeutic help as a conclusion to the subject of not avoiding your triggers but facing them in a bid to deflate the notion of a threat that they pose.

Exposure therapy does not encourage your behavior of avoidance. You may decide to drive thousands of miles because of your fear of flying or stay at home and miss your friend's farewell party because of your social phobia. Through exposure therapy, you start a step-by-step process to face your fears.

You are not thrown into the deep end immediately; your therapist will guide you and gradually encourage you to face the fear that is your trigger. There are three stages to exposure therapy.

- **In-vivo**—facing your fears directly by confronting them. You will be asked to address a gathering if you are dealing with a social phobia.

- **Imagining**—this exposure makes you imagine you are experiencing the incident that is causing your anxiety. If you are dealing with PTSD and an emotional trigger related to the incident, your therapist will ask you to imagine yourself in that traumatic situation.

- **Flooding**—you are exposed to your fears and triggers, beginning with the most traumatic, where you are thrown into the deep end to instigate your natural survival ability. Or in this case, the therapist will help you to deal with the emotional trigger deflating its hold on you.

Before therapy begins, you must list your identified anxieties and triggers. The therapist will then work through each one. You will be required to concentrate and spend time confronting the fears until they lose their power over you—that will be your goal, and you will be assisted and encouraged to get there.

Before you begin your journey, your therapist will introduce you to a coping mechanism. You will learn deep breathing techniques to help you relax; practice and use them to calm down when you start confronting your anxieties.

Cognitive Behavioral Therapy (CBT)

CBT is the most popular of all behavior therapy methods; one principal factor being it addresses several mental health disorders, from panic attacks to GAD. The theory on which CBT works is simple. Therapy suggests your reactions or behavior to a situation is governed by your thoughts and the emotions that thought promotes. The situation does not influence your behavior—mind over matter is what CBT is looking at teaching you.

The method uses negative thoughts and behavior to analyze and understand your thinking process and final emotion. The examination is conducted across two main factors that link thought and mood with behavior.

- Cognitive therapy, as the name suggests, explores your cognitive distortions and how negativity affects your behavior compared to your situation. Are your thoughts governing your reaction or the situation?

- Behavior therapy analyzes your behavior through your reactions when faced with an emotional trigger or anxiety.

Through analysis, CBT can show you how your negative thoughts are generating negative emotions and behavior from you.

Let's say your partner wants to take you out for dinner for no apparent reason, and you think they must love and cherish you. Those thoughts generate a happy mood. You become loving and appreciative toward your partner.

But, if you think, "my partner finally decided to appreciate me and show they care," your mood is one of apprehension where you are not overly happy or sad. You merely go with the flow, thinking— "well, it's about time I was appreciated."

Lastly, if you think the out-of-the-blue dinner treat was because your partner is guilty of something, you will generate feelings of anger, which will reflect in your behavior, where you look tense and angry because you are trying to show them you know something is wrong.

Do you see how different emotions generated for the same situation can make you feel opposite emotions? That is what CBT will reveal and will try to help you change your general thinking process. You will be taught that the glass is half full and not half empty.

Cognitive restructuring, which we discussed before, occurs through the therapy offered via CBT treatment. The treatment works by identifying your negative thinking process and then dissecting those thoughts to challenge their validity, after which those negative and often unrealistic thoughts are replaced with more feasible ideas.

Your negative and disruptive thought is taken, analyzed, and replaced with a more realistic view.

- Negative thought— *No one will talk to me because I am new if I go to the party.*

- Realistic thought— *Going to the party will be an excellent opportunity to get to know a few people and introduce myself.*

In the process, you will also be helped with and taught how to use more positive thought processes to cope with triggers, recognize your anxieties, and face them, thereby rendering them powerless.

Psychotherapy—Talk Therapy

The main aim of psychotherapy is to help you avoid or control your negative thoughts and self-talk. Psychotherapy helps with various mental health disorders and works by teaching you to cope with trauma, emotional triggers, panic disorders, depression, and other disturbing situations that can lead to depression. The healing you receive through these methods will change depending on the type of anxiety you are dealing with and may sometimes include the combination of medicine and other forms of behavior therapy.

Psychotherapy works on the premise of honest talk, which helps a bond to form between you and your therapist. The method, similar to counseling but with a more open and trustworthy analysis, can be between a group of people or just one. The sessions comprise of sharing private and intimate details about your problems. Therefore, privacy is guaranteed together with respect for personal space. At no point, no matter how close you feel to the therapist, are you encouraged to engage in physical touch, a natural reaction to the closeness one feels to another person who seems sensitive and interested—a common trait when dealing with insecurities and anxious thoughts.

Psychotherapy is available in various methods to treat different mental health disorders.

- Interpersonal therapy—this is not a long-term treatment method because you will be shown how to identify anxieties between people—partners, family, friends, office coworkers, etcetera. Through interpersonal therapy, you can learn to communicate your feelings with others more effectively and resolve underlying issues such as a switch in your role at work, unresolved grief, conflicts and grudges you may harbor against others, and disagreements waiting to bubble over. Learn to interact positively with people through clear communication, with your emotions in check.

- Psychodynamic therapy—analyzes triggers and fears that could have developed due to childhood trauma or incidents. The method addresses your repetitive pattern of negative thoughts while helping you build self-awareness.

- Supportive therapy—as the name suggests, you will be taught to cope with your anxieties by introducing you to establish coping mechanisms that help the type of mental health issue with which you are dealing.

- CBT, too, is a type of psychotherapy

Identifying and Choosing to Face and Conquer Your Emotional Triggers Will Reward You with a Healthy Relationship

So—how does taking charge of your emotional triggers help to improve your relationship?

The success of a relationship is based on how well you communicate and the level of respect you show each other. Often, a person dealing with anxiety and emotional triggers will find it hard to meet those markers.

Identifying and taking charge of your emotional triggers will help you to breathe new life into your relationship. Your newfound self-worth will reflect in the thoughts, emotions, and behavior you associate with your relationship.

Solving your social anxieties will help you become a wholesome part of your partner's life, actively take part, and savor the stresses that come with a committed relationship.

Couples counseling is an ideal method to air your confusion, thoughts, and graveness; it is an open forum where you can learn to change your negative thoughts to more practical ones. Next, look at one of the most accessible forms of control for your anxiety—breathing.

CHAPTER 5

— · —

BREATH IN—BREATH OUT!

So the next time someone is scared and feels like

they can't breathe, shaking and crying, unable to see,

don't tell them they're overreacting; don't call them crazy. —Tiffaney L Ganci (Ganci, 2018)

You can use breathing to control your triggers and anxiety. An act that takes place as automatic reflex, breathing fills our lungs with oxygen and helps rejuvenate our cells. From calming an increased heart rate to stilling sudden anxious thoughts, breathing can be your most helpful tool for controlling anxiety. This chapter will examine breathing exercises to help you manage your triggers and anxieties.

Amanda Seyfried Talks About Panic Attacks

By now, you understand that anxiety and mental health disorders are not limited to social standing or how important you are; anyone is vulnerable, and Amanda Seyfried is no different. The talented actress describes panic attacks as life-or-death experiences where the fight or flight mode puts the body into overdrive—to crash at the end, leaving you exhausted.

Amanda has admitted to seeking help for anxiety disorders from her teenage years, more importantly for her obsessive-compulsive disorders. She insists that mental health diseases are taken just as seriously as other physical illnesses, stating that although it is not a physically visible illness, the impact and implications are just as severe. At the same time, Amanda admits to being on antidepressants since she was 19 years of age (Harper, 2021). Let's look at other methods too that will aid you with controlling your anxiety.

Breathing for Relief

Have you noticed how your breathing changes with your emotions? Accelerated and shallow breathing often represents anger, excitement, and fear. Or, if you feel happy and content, you tend to take long, deep breaths—sighs of relief that signal calmness. That is the type of breathing you must aim for whenever anxiety or triggers threaten you—deep, calm breaths to instill a sense of peace.

Deep breathing works by influencing your autoimmune nervous response. This system comprises two factors; the parasympathetic nervous system, which functions on affecting your reflexes for relaxation, and the other is your sympathetic nervous system which influences your fight or flight reaction. Through deep breathing, you aim to increase the impact your parasympathetic response has on your mind, thus helping you to calm down.

How to Use Deep Breathing to Calm Your Body and Mind

If you mimic fast, short, and shallow breathing, you will automatically induce a sensation of stress in conjunction with your elevated heart rate. Likewise, you can learn to calm a racing heart associated with anxiety and panic by practicing deep breathing.

Deep breathing is the process of breathing through your stomach. Deep long breaths fill your lungs with air and bloat up your stomach. Practice deep breathing by placing your hand on your stomach and then taking a deep breath until you see your hand rise. Hold your breath for a count of three and breathe out. Recite the mantra as I have explained in chapter 3, under "Tips to Start Your Day on A Positive Vibe."

Lower Your Stress and Learn to Relax with Deep Breathing

Through this experiment, learn the art of calming down with deep breathing; sit or stand in a quiet spot, close your eyes, and imagine a stressful event to increase your heart rate and activate your sympathetic nervous response. Start deep breathing and let the feeling of relaxation wash over you. You will have to practice a few times to feel comfortable with the technique, but once you do, you can do deep breathing to calm down and deal with triggers anywhere at any time.

Breathwork to Help Lower Your Anxiety

Through several methods, you can practice breathing exercises or breathwork to calm and comfort your mind. Let me introduce you to the popular few that are easy to learn and practice.

Square Breathing/Box Breathing/4 Part Breath/4x4 Breathing

This breathing method can help you change your mood by connecting with your mind, body, and nervous system to calm down and deal with anxiety.

How to Begin

- Preferably sit in a straight-back chair and lean back.

Ground your feet by placing them flat on the ground to feel the floor pressing up against the soles. Become conscious of the chair and how it is supporting you.

- Slowly exhale and feel your lungs deflate, then gently breathe in on a count of four through your nose.

- Hold your breath for a count of four

- Exhale on a count of four through your mouth

- When you come to the end of the exhale, hold it to a count of four.

- Use an image to center your breathing. If you imagine a square, then use the pauses between exhaling and inhaling to move from one plane to the next so your breathing moves around the square.

Square breathing can help reduce stress and anxiety. Or to feel more inspired and focused and for clarity when making important decisions. You can practice this breathing method anywhere, whenever you feel overly anxious or face a challenging situation such as arguments with your partner or work-related stresses.

Belly Breathing or Diaphragmatic Breathing

The diaphragm at the base of your lungs is an important muscle that, aided by your stomach muscles, empties your lungs of air, thus, encouraging fresh air flow.

This breathing technique helps strengthen the diaphragm, reduces your need for oxygen, and makes breathing easier and less effortless. Diaphragmatic breathing helps to increase your lung capacity fully and requires less energy for the breathing process.

Improve a range of illnesses with diaphragmatic breathing. Stress, anxiety, asthma, and chronic obstructive pulmonary disease (COPD) are conditions that inhibit the function of the diaphragm.

Diaphragm breathing helps improve the following:

- Blood pressure

- Stabilizes or reduces your heart rate

- Optimizes muscle usage during physical exertion

- Aids your lungs to detoxify by releasing waste as well as gas

- You can learn to relax and de-stress

How to Practice Belly Breathing

- Lay flat on the floor, or on your bed. Add a pillow to support your head. Bend your knees and add support under your knees if you like.

- Place your hand on your diaphragm. You should then be able to feel your diaphragm rise and fall as you breathe.

- Just like in deep breathing, take a breath, and watch your hand rise as your diaphragm/stomach expands.

- Exhale through closed lips slowly and watch as your hand on your belly drops. Contract your stomach muscles as you breathe out.

- Throughout all the processes, the hand on your chest should remain still to ensure you breathe through your diaphragm.

By practicing, you can easily use this breathing method to calm your anxieties; at first, it may seem complicated, but it will soon become a valuable coping tool once you get it right.

Relaxing Breath or 4–7–8 Breathing

Relaxing breath is an exact breathing technique that stems from yoga and helps you to stay calm and keep your anxieties at bay. The method is also a favored aid for falling asleep due to its rhythmic breathing pattern. The 4–7–8 breathing pattern works by taking four seconds to inhale, seven seconds to hold that breath, and eight seconds to exhale slowly.

The method is beneficial for sleep and getting your emotions in check by helping calm your emotional responses. The same theory applies to controlling your impulses and cravings, where using the 4–7–8 breathing technique will help you to practice more restraint and avoid giving into thoughtless and sudden needs.

Practicing the 4–7–8 Breathing Technique

- Begin by exhaling and letting out the air from your lungs

- Then inhale through your nose and breathe for a count of four seconds.

- Hold that breath for seven seconds

- Breathe to a count of eight seconds, force the air through your semi-closed month and make a sound like—whoosh.

- You can keep the steps going for at least four counts as part of your training, and before long, you will master the art of 4–7–8 breathing whenever you start feeling overwhelmed.

Using Breathing Exercises to Calm Down has Positive Impacts on Relationships

Mindfulness breathing is an exercise that helps you to calm down, heightens your senses, and allows you to clarify and see your life from a positive perspective. Therefore, no one is better than your partner in practicing breathing exercises.

Using the intimacy of practicing deep breathing together to deepen your relationship will help you to overcome inhibitions and fears. Someone with commitment phobias or any other anxious tendency that prevent them from forming proper bonds, by learning to trust, can learn emotional self-regulation and take control of their emotions, thoughts, and behavior. You can become fully aware of your partner and see them in a new light, free from the negative thoughts that block you from accepting and becoming satisfied with your relationship. Through a heightened awareness of your partner, during the Mindfulness breathing sessions, you will be reminded of what first attracted you to them.

Learn to appreciate your partner and show gratitude—without your anxieties blocking your perspective. Become sensitive to your partner's nature and learn to think beyond your worries—develop empathy within your relationship.

You will be able to block out stresses, worries, and negative panic to focus on each other's presence and be in that moment when you can connect, forming a bond free from the chronic anxieties that hold you back from giving your relationship a 100%.

Did you know that your diet greatly influences your mental health— "you are what you eat" is an adage that rings true in this case. The quality of the food you eat can significantly influence your mind. Let's learn more about the gut-brain axis and foods that trigger anxiety.

CHAPTER 6

— • —

DON'T FEED YOUR ANXIETY

*B*ecause I know I am more than just my anxiety,

and one day I hope to be free of it entirely. —Tiffaney L Ganci (Ganci, 2018)

Choosing to eat healthy is a wise move toward your overall well-being. Eating wholesome and healthy foods will ensure you deal with fewer mood fluctuations and loss of focus with a happier and healthier outlook on life.

You will be surprised to learn the close connection diet has with anxiety; in truth, your anxiety feeds off your diet. So, let's look at starving that anxiety!

Selma Blair Held on to Anxiety Until it Exploded

Anxiety affects anyone disregarding who they are and what they do. Anxiety is also highly treatable with many ways to safeguard yourself from constant worry and panic. Actress Selma Blair admitted to dealing with postpartum depression, alcohol addiction, and anxiety for many years until a public outburst on a plane finally made her realize and seek help. The actress describes the incident as "humbling" and a time when she "fell apart" (Dawn, 2018).

No one should wait that long to seek help. As we are about to learn, you can start to change your well-being and heal with simple changes like diet, which significantly impacts your mental health.

The Food You Eat and Your Emotional Moods Swings

Do you eat to compensate for your mood? Or treat yourself with food as a reward?

Did you stop to think that "rewarding" yourself with food is only necessary because you don't usually eat that type of food—and why is that? Perhaps the food is not the correct type of nourishment for you.

There is a difference between nutrition-dense foods and calorie-dense foods. The latter is harmful and can impact both your mental and physical well-being. Eating calorie-dense foods—added sugars, simple carbs, and unhealthy fats can put what is known as your gut-brain axis off balance.

What is the Gut-Brain Axis?

Nearly 60% of people with mental health issues are diagnosed with an imbalance in their gut health (Liu & Zhu, 2018). This imbalance happens within your gut microbiome, consisting of billions of bacteria (micro-organisms) that aid digestion and influence the secretion of hormones because of their connection and constant communication with your brain. The gut microbiota also called your gut flora, has both good and bad bugs. A balance of more good bugs than bad must ensure your overall health. Food can often put this balance off; when bad bugs increase, you develop physical and mental illnesses.

Your gut microbiota forms neural links with your brain, immune and endocrine system (neuro-endocrine-immune pathways), known as the gut-brain axis (GBA). The food you eat reacts differently from your gut microbiota, which influences your gut-brain axis. In short, your anxiety and mood swings are often related to what you eat and the influence on your gut bacteria, where several hormones that form a connection with your brain are produced. These hormones link with your neurological system to ensure several functions take place smoothly.

Serotonin, important for regulating mood, is mainly produced in the gut. Over 95% of serotonin is produced in your gut (Terry & Margolis, 2017). Gut health is an invaluable link to your mental health.

Feel Good Foods That are Bad for Your Gut

Food can cause an imbalance of your gut bacteria, leading to mental health problems such as stress, anxiety, and depression. Because the good bacteria constantly communicates with your endocrine system and brain, a decrease can disrupt your hormone production and lead to mood swings. Some food types can cause a sudden spike in feel-good hormones, while others will give you a sudden rush of energy. All those are short-lived changes in your mood with damaging side effects.

Sugar is one of the substances that should be limited for a good reason—it feeds the harmful bacteria in your gut microbiota. Sugar is food for harmful gut bacteria, and constantly indulging in food containing added sugars will lead to an imbalance and gut problems such as irritable bowel disease (IBS). IBS is closely related to patients developing GAD and other anxiety disorders (Zamani et al., 2019). IBS is a common disease of the gastrointestinal tract with symptoms of abdominal pain and irregularity of bowel movements.

You may crave some foods that, once eaten, activate your reward system, which releases dopamine, a temporary feel-good hormone linked to several mental health disorders, including ADHD.

Dopamine rush can become addictive and is linked to obesity and other eating disorders, addictions, and anxiety. When you eat something you like, the brain reacts by releasing dopamine. And because you enjoy the rush of euphoria that follows, you crave the feeling more, rewarding yourself with food that triggers the release of dopamine until the brain decides to deregulate the hormone levels it determines are too much.

Low dopamine levels lead to anxiety disorders such as depression and a lack of motivation; Parkinson's and Schizophrenia are other conditions that may occur as dopamine deficiency.

Food Types to Avoid

Before you begin your revolutionized eating pattern that will change your overall well-being, it's best to clear out your pantry of the temptations—food that can cause harm. Here is a list of foods that can aggravate your anxiety, do no good for your overall health, and are best left out of your healthy eating pattern.

- Sugar

Besides causing tooth decay, diabetes, high blood sugar, and insulin resistance, sugar and products containing added sugars can increase anxiety, depression, and mood swings. Energy spikes brought on by an increase in blood sugar drop soon after the sugar levels decrease. You are left with an energy slump, mood alterations, and a craving for more sugar. If you continue to feed those cravings, the constant pattern of highs and lows leads to an increase in cortisol, the stress hormone, and adrenaline which can induce panic and anxiety.

Sugar is present in its natural form as lactose in milk, fructose in fruits and vegetables, and glucose in plant food. When sugars are extracted from their natural source and processed, they become refined sugar.

Dextrose, maltose, cane sugar, corn syrup, and maple syrup are all added sugars. Refined sugars are extracted from sugar cane, corn, and sugar beets and are just as bad. Honey, although a naturally occurring sugar, is classified as an added sugar when added to food containing sugars.

Doughnuts, frosting, cakes, and all sorts of sugary foods that contain added sugars fall into this category and are best left alone.

- Fruit juice

Fruits contain fructose, a natural sugar, and the fiber needed for healthy gut microbiota. Fiber is a super food for your gut bacteria and digestive process. However, when you make fruit juice and discard the pulp, you throw out all the fiber. What is left is a high-sugar drink. Make sure to eat whole fruits and vegetables as a part of your healthy diet and avoid juices.

- Simple carb foods

Simple carb foods are carbohydrates that have been refined. White rice or grain from which the bran has been stripped, white flour, and any sugar that is not in its natural form. All simple carbs can cause an almost instantaneous spike in your blood sugar.

White bread, pastries, and cakes are all types of simple carbs—yes, even toast made from white bread is bad for your anxiety.

- Light sauces, marinades, and dressings

These garnishes can contain large amounts of sugar, which will be disguised as added sugars as they contain high fructose corn syrup or other added sugars. Even more disturbing is the "light" version of sauces, dressings, and marinades, which contain aspartame, an artificial sweetener. Aspartame is linked to an increase in anxiety and depression symptoms. More precisely, the substance is linked to cognitive and behavioral problems, insomnia, anxiety, mood swings, and depression (Lindseth et al., 2014).

Soy sauce contains gluten and can have side effects if you are gluten intolerant, as it can act on your anxiety, making you feel lethargic and unmotivated.

- Processed foods

Processed meat, canned foods, and even some processed cheese all contain high levels of added salt. The extra salt will increase your blood pressure, which in turn causes your heart to work faster. When the heart rate elevates, adrenaline is released, leading to an increase in panic and anxiety.

Some processed food packaged in plastic containers or cans lined with a substance known as bisphenol A (BPA) has been found to affect anxiety. This is especially high risk for pregnant women and young children as the chemical can cause anxiety very early (Perera et al., 2016).

- Caffeine-containing products

We already explored the effects of caffeine on anxiety as an emotional trigger in chapter 4; coffee and energy drinks are both high in caffeine and will cause dependency and withdrawal symptoms. Gradually reduce your coffee intake and try switching to decaf. Energy drinks are double the trouble as, apart from high levels of caffeine, they contain many sugars, either refined or artificial, and both are anxiety triggers.

- Industrial seed oils

Industrial seed or processed vegetable oils made through mass production are bad for your overall health. Apart from being linked to heart disease and macular degeneration, to name a few, industrial seed oils contain a high ratio of omega-6 fatty acids. While this is essential for your health, the levels in industrial seed oils are too high. Omega-3 and -6 essential oils offer several health benefits, but omega-3 essential fatty acids are the most needed for your cognitive health and vision. The ratio between omega-3 and omega-6 should be 4:1, ideally; however, industrial seed oils can raise the omega-6 to omega-3 ratio to 16:1, which is the norm in our modern diets (Simopoulos, 2006).

Omega-6 oils can lead to inflammation, which can cause a leaky gut and affect the delicate balance of your gut microbiota. It can also contain trans fats, especially margarine made from industrial seed oils, which are hydrogenated—a process rendering the oil solid at room temperature. Trans fats have been linked to memory and cognitive decline and as a trigger for anxiety and depression (DiNicolantonio & O'Keefe, 2018). Avoid fried foods, especially junk food loaded with industrial seed oils. Frosting and pastry, too, are high in refined sugars and hydrogenated oils (margarine, shortening).

- Alcohol

One drink for women and two for men is the allowed percentage of alcoholic beverages per day. However, if your anxiety and panic increase, you will benefit from total abstinence from alcohol. Not only will the drink disrupt your sleep patterns, but it can also cause a loss of focus. While alcohol in moderation is considered a de-stressor, it can have the opposite effect when it acts on your central nervous system if you are dealing with anxiety. In such instances, you can become overly drowsy, have fewer inhibitions, and become prone to making risky and harmful judgments.

- Additives

Monosodium glutamate, aspartame, certain food dyes, etc., are some additives and flavor enhancers often included in the food. Such additives can aggravate anxiety, induce mood fluctuations, and alter behavior (Bartels et al., 2008).

A good rule of thumb for purchasing food is to check the nutrition facts labels on packaged food. They contain all the information you need including percentages of sugar, added sugars, fats, trans fats, additives, and other nutritional values such as carbohydrates, fiber, etcetera.

What Should I Eat for Mental and Physical Well-being?

Whole foods are the best. Fresh nutrition dense foods containing the right amounts of macro and micronutrients will help improve your overall well-being. Macronutrients include carbohydrates, proteins, and fats, while micronutrients are minerals and vitamins.

Eat plenty of:

- Whole carbs—food rich in fiber such as whole grains; brown rice, oats, quinoa, barley, fresh vegetables, dark green leafy vegetables, potatoes, and fruits

- Good fats—avocado, coconut, and olive oil, as well as fatty fish rich in omega-3 essential oils needed for cognitive health.

- Protein—eggs, lean red meat, chicken, chickpeas, soy, and green peas

- Minerals—iron, zinc, magnesium-rich food; eggs, beans, cocoa, avocado, organ meat, shellfish, pulses, nuts, and cruciferous vegetables

- Vitamins—fruits, vegetables, and berries

Foods That Benefit Mental Health

Transitioning to a wholesome and nutrient-rich diet will significantly impact your overall well-being. Here is a list of foods that have been scientifically proven to have a particularly positive effect on your mental well-being.

- Brazil nuts

Contain a chemical called selenium, which is beneficial in reducing chronic inflammation; a condition often present during anxiety (Thomson et al., 2008). Selenium is also an antioxidant, as is vitamin E, which too is found in Brazil nuts. A lack of vitamin E is linked to anxiety conditions in children. Make sure you do not exceed the daily allowed value of selenium; the limit is 400 mg which amounts to around 3–4 nuts daily.

- Eggs

A rich source of protein, eggs are one of the few foods high in vitamin D, an essential nutrient that aids calcium absorption. Tryptophan, one of the amino acids, is also found in protein-rich eggs. Tryptophan influences the secretion of serotonin, one of your feel-good hormones, thus regulating your brain function, mood, sleep patterns, and behavior.

- Fatty Fish

Fatty fish is considered brain food, one of the best sources of omega-3 fatty acids. Omega-3 fatty acids contain eicosapentaenoic acid (EPA) and docosahexaenoic acid (DHA). These long-chain polyunsaturated fatty acids are present more in fish and shellfish. DHA and EPA aid with fetal, cognitive, and retinal development. Studies confirm the benefits of DHA and EPA on anxiety (Natacci et al, 2018).

- Turmeric

Curcumin, a substance found in turmeric, helps reduce inflammation and oxidative stress, which occurs when there is an imbalance of free radicals and antioxidants in your body. When free radicals increase, they can cause cell damage and induce inflammation. Curcumin reduces oxidative stress, mood fluctuations, anxiety, and depression (Fusar-Poli et al., 2019).

Turmeric is a popular spice in South Asian cuisine; you can reap the benefits of turmeric by choosing to enjoy a glass of warm turmeric milk at night. Choose a recipe from the many available online.

- Dark Chocolate

It contains polyphenols, among which flavonoids are the most beneficial (Al Sunni & Latif, 2014). The substance is identified with reduced neural inflammation and improved blood transfusion to the brain. Tryptophan amino acid is found in chocolate which induces the production of serotonin. The mineral magnesium is found in dark chocolate, which is often a prescribed supplement for dealing with anxiety.

- Chamomile Tea

This relaxing herbal tea is drunk across the world as a calming and soothing drink, especially before bedtime. Chamomile has several good properties as an antioxidant and antibacterial agent. As per a study, 1,500 mg of chamomile, when taken daily, positively reduced anxiety (Amsterdam et al., 2019).

- Green Tea

It contains theanine, an amino acid associated with reducing anxiety. The substance helps ease tension and mood alterations and offers the benefits of relaxing and calming your mind (Williams et al., 2019).

Dietary Supplements That Make a Difference in the Fight Against Anxiety

Before we end this section on foods that benefit anxiety, it's important to note specific compounds that positively affect your mental well-being. They are substances found in the food mentioned earlier that offer an added benefit to managing your anxiety better.

- EPA and DHA

Both substances have positive influences on your neurotransmitters. Found mainly in omega-3 fatty acids, EPA and DHA reduce inflammation; a diet rich in these long-chain fatty acids will aid in lowering neural inflammation. Eating a diet rich in both substances is important as EPA is fast metabolized and diminishes quickly, while DHA reserves tend to reduce with age. Therefore, paying particular attention to how much DHA and EPA you get through your diet is important. If you feel there is an absence, check with your healthcare provider about supplementing on omega-3 fatty acids.

- Alpha-tocopherol

One of the eight components of vitamin E, alpha-tocopherol is an antioxidant and anti-inflammatory compound that helps fight free radicals and inflammation and is beneficial for controlling anxiety. An essential nutrient for your immune system to function, this component of vitamin aids with the development of your neurological system too. Seeds, hazelnuts, almonds, sunflower seeds, other nuts, and healthy oils like sunflower and coconut oil, while wheatgerm oil contains the highest numbers. A lack of alpha-tocopherol during pregnancy can lead to neural disorders in the fetus.

- Folic acid

Folate or folic acid is a water-soluble B9 vitamin. B vitamins are essential for your metabolism. When metabolized, folic acid becomes L-methyl folate. It can then influence the secretion of your feel-good hormones serotonin, dopamine, and norepinephrine, essential for the healthy function of your mental state. Include plenty of beans, dark green leafy vegetables such as kale, spinach, broccoli and peanuts, seafood, liver, whole grains, and fresh fruits in your diet for a good supply of folate.

- Magnesium

An essential mineral in the fight against anxiety—magnesium is an anti-inflammatory. According to recent studies, magnesium may improve your brain function, which found that the mineral has anti-neural inflammatory properties. Magnesium may influence your hypothalamus, an organ located at the back of your brain that regulates the secretion of hormones and thus controls your moods (Boyle et al., 2017). Check with your healthcare provider about the appropriate type of magnesium to supplement as an aid for your anxiety. In the meantime, you can increase your intake of spinach, seeds, nuts, and legumes, rich sources of essential minerals.

Other Essential Macronutrients for Mental Health

- Micronutrient – Benefits to Mental Health

- Calcium – Helps improve and maintain the chemical signal process between your brain and cells. Aids with the release of neurotransmitters.

- Vitamin D -Aid with serotonin manufacture

- Vitamin B – Helps synthesize neurotransmitters. B1 functions are similar to acetylcholine, a chemical in the brain that aids with memory, focus, and learning, among other functions.

- Vitamin B2 – An essential antioxidant, B2 helps metabolize essential fatty acids in the brain, such as omega 3.

- Vitamin B3 – Niacin and B3 act like an antidepressant and help improve cell function in the brain.

- Vitamin B6 – Helps synthesize neurotransmitters

- Vitamin B12 – Helps prevent brain atrophy, leading to neurons and memory loss.

- Zinc - Essential for brain development, zinc is a vital micro for mental health. Zinc improves short- and long-term memory and helps with protein synthesis in the brain.

- Iron – Aids with brain function and development. It may improve learning deficiencies and memory loss. Helps with the metabolization of neurotransmitters.

Choose Healthy Sleep as Part of Your Transition

Make it a point to get a good night's sleep; knock off the television, tablet, smartphone, and computer at least an hour before bed-time. The screens emit blue light, which inhibits the production of melatonin, a hormone that induces sleep, and the last thing you need is to develop or feed a sleeping disorder.

Choose to stay well hydrated by drinking enough liquids. Most of your main organs, your brain, heart, liver, kidneys, and lungs, are made up of high percentages of water, and for their optimal func-tion, you need to keep them hydrated. Your brain, for example, is almost 80% water (Water Science School, 2019). Adult women should consume about 2.3 quarts (2.2 liters) of water daily.

There is a close link between sleep and anxiety. Unhealthy sleep habits can lead to stress and the development of mental health diseases, while conversely, mental health conditions can also cause sleep problems.

Did you know that sleeping is a coping mechanism for anxiety?

A good seven- to eight-hour sleep will help you to rejuvenate your body and mind and increase your focus. Naps too, when enjoyed in moderation (preferably for around half an hour), can help you to improve your mood by giving your mind a break. However, long sleep durations and constant napping may indicate you are deal-ing with depression and stress. If that is the case, avoid indulging in too much sleep and choose physical exercise.

Improve Your Relationship by Starting a Healthy Eating Pattern Together

As a couple, there are several activities you can initiate together; a dietary change is one of the best. Learning to take care of your body as a joint effort makes the transition easy with a partner.

Choose to eat healthy by establishing goals and targets to achieve at the end of a set period.

Make your grocery list together and choose wholesome ingredients that appeal to you both. Compromise and select recipes that serve both your tastes. Shop for groceries together and experiment with new ingredients with the potential to improve your mental and physical well-being. Make the transition to a healthier diet a joint effort and not one forced on the other, and you can guarantee both success and an enjoyable experience.

Match your moods and avoid being lazy and anxious because of eating the wrong type of food. Enjoy the improved energy levels and healthy hormone secretion that eating the proper diet can accomplish.

Next, let's look at enhancing your health by including healthy activities to improve your physical fitness and give your mind the boost it needs to fight anxiety.

CHAPTER 7

— · —

SWEAT IT OUT

I am stronger than this. I am stronger than my anxiety—Tiffaney L Ganci (Ganci, 2018)

Exercise or physical activity is just as important for a healthy mind and body as eating a healthy diet. A combination of both can improve your chances of mental health success beyond medication, as the practice will help establish a long-term healthy lifestyle. Let's complete your transition to a healthier and fuller lifestyle by looking at physical activity options that can help you cope with your anxiety more successfully.

Missy Elliot Says Anxiety Is not a Temporary Worry

Anxiety certainly is not a temporary worry and deserves all your attention. Acknowledging your condition as one that needs to be looked after and treated will point you toward the path to success. Missy Elliot has known the gravity of dealing with anxiety for many years and admits to feeling overwhelmed and suffering a severe panic attack before her performance at the 2015 Super Bowl; the attack warranted medical help and intravenous treatment (IV). She was willing to get over the anxiety on the day of her performance and did so (Nast, 2015).

Fighting back and resolving to get back to a semblance of normal routine is crucial for recovery. No matter how bleak and dark the days seem, facing each day with enthusiasm, the sun in your face will activate chemicals that give your mood a boost and new confidence to "get over" your anxiety. Sweat it out and lighten the load!

The Benefits of Exercise for Anxiety

Exercise or any form of regular physical activity can help boost your mood and reduce stress, panic, and feelings of anxiety. When you engage in physical activity, chemical reactions occur in your brain, encouraging the secretion of hormones, especially norepinephrine and serotonin. Physical activity also promotes the secretion of endorphins which are pain busters adding to your feelings of relaxed calm.

- Exercise can help increase self-confidence

Exercise can help you lose weight and feel good about yourself. The release of feel-good hormones will encourage a sense of calm, improve your mood, and energize your body to enhance cognition functions, all of which boost your self-confidence by getting rid of negative thoughts and depressive thinking.

- Exercise improves endurance

Exercise improves blood flow to your organs and boosts their performance. The action improves your heart and lung perfor-mance, strengthening your endurance and aiding you with more prolonged bouts of activity without feeling tired.

- Enjoy better sleep with exercise

Exercise can help you to fall asleep faster. As long as you don't exercise too close to bedtime and end up all pumped up and energized, physical activity can help you fall into a deeper sleep faster.

- Lower your risk of common illnesses

Staying active and healthy will lower your chances of developing chronic diseases such as type 2 diabetes, high blood pressure, cardiovascular ailments, stroke, arthritis, depression, and anxiety. Exercise can boost levels of your good cholesterol, HDL, and get rid of fatty deposits in the blood called triglycerides and levels of LDL, the bad cholesterol.

- Improves your mental health

Exercise promotes brain health; increased blood flow takes essential oxygen to the brain, improving its function, thus stimulating the health of your brain cells, and encouraging the secretion of hormones necessary for maintaining your mental health. Exercise can help relieve inflammation and oxidative stress, which is essential to prevent brain cell decomposition as you age.

Some studies even prove an improvement in the size of the hippocampus, a section of the brain that aids with learning and memory, thus boosting mental functions, especially since the hippocampus decreases in size as you age (Erickson et al., 2011).

Best Exercises to Conquer Your Anxiety

Here is a list of the best exercises to help you with your anxiety.

- Swimming

Swimming helps relieve stress and is an enjoyable activity that offers you the benefit of water therapy. Water can help relieve mental and body stress, while the swimming action is rhythmical and soothing.

Boost brain health by being immersed in water, which promotes blood flow, nutrients to the brain, and glucose, the brain's primary energy source.

Swimming encourages the release of endorphins and is an excellent way to release anxiety and feel good about yourself. Studies claim swimming makes people happier and less stressed (Safari et al., 2020), especially when you choose to swim at a club where you can interact with others and enjoy relaxed conversations.

- Walking and jogging

Did you know that walking or jogging is an off switch for your anxiety?

When going on a walk or jog, the portion of the brain that controls anxiety takes a break. The amygdala is the part of your brain that controls your decision-making, and it works based on one task at a time, which makes walking one of the best exercises for concentrating on a specific task.

Open spaces are best for walks, although city dwellers will benefit from brisk walks in the mornings or evenings to get their heart, blood, and oxygen pumping. Weekend hikes to explore nature will work wonders for your mental health. Viewing nature and beautiful scenes have been linked to the release of oxytocin, the love or bonding hormone which makes us want to connect with others.

- Biking

Biking is a stimulating activity that can quickly improve your mood and replace your anxiety with a sense of adventure. Biking takes you places; it gets you out of the house and takes you on an adventure across beautiful country scenes or exploring different parts of the city. You can choose to bike and explore or indulge in a quick cardio workout by biking daily for a specific time. Cardio workouts that happen through activities like biking have proven to be beneficial for anxiety by boosting mood and reducing anxiety. People who enjoy biking have lower levels of stress.

- Dancing

Nothing helps you forget your inhibitions and have a good time, like dancing. The activity not only releases endorphins and serotonin but is a great way to learn to socialize and enjoy a cardio workout in the process.

Dancing is an excellent hobby to adopt, especially when you dislike regular exercise. You can easily enroll in a dance class to help you ease out of your stressful situation and enjoy a few hours of uninhibited fun.

Dancing is so effective against anxiety that the American Dance Therapy Association calls dancing "the psychotherapeutic use of movement to further the emotional, cognitive, physical and social integration of the individual." (Winters Fisher, 2019). Dancing is highly beneficial for you if you suffer from trauma or PTSD; dance therapy can successfully address childhood trauma.

How Can Exercise and Physical Activity Help Your Relationship?

Exercising increases your heart rate and makes you breathe faster as you feel that sudden rush of excitement. Exercising together can strengthen your bond, amp up your attraction to each other, increase your sex drive and add excitement to your relationship.

Participating in physically exertive activities together increases awareness and attraction between couples. The exercises I have listed are all ideal for enjoying with a partner, giving you plenty of opportunities to bond and enjoy the great outdoors or have fun as a couple.

Not to be forgotten is the thrill of working out without someone else. It sure beats the boredom of exercising alone. Having your partner with you when that rush of excitement and invigoration hits is a boost to your relationship.

Anxiety can be controlled through sheer determination, establishing goals, and lifestyle changes. One more facet to look at and our muse for this chapter, Missy Elliot, reveals that aspect well through her quote: "I know it was nothing but the grace of God that lifted me up and took me through that performance" (Lukas, n.d.).

Missy Elliot talks about faith—I want to introduce you to spirituality, a much broader belief than religion. Let's look at how spirituality can help your anxiety.

CHAPTER 8

— · —

TURN TO SPIRITUALITY

*H*elp them realize there is more to life than this misery,

and no matter the doubt inside, they will be who they

are meant to be.

Breathe. I will get through this. —Tiffaney L Ganci (Ganci, 2018)

Spirituality is based on trust and faith in a higher power, a belief that helps us to place our worries and concerns in the care of something far greater than our comprehension, with nothing but faith keeping us hoping for a positive result.

Spirituality cannot be compartmentalized or labeled. It is not a religion or a practice but a way of life. It touches us through different angles, paths, beliefs, and experiences. Seeing wonder in nature, having faith in a religion, and your purpose in life are all aspects of spirituality that keeps you grounded and within parameters that help shape your life through the chaos.

That is precisely what you must provide for your anxiety, a way to understand the chaos—the erratic thoughts, panic, worries, and uncontrollable behavior. Let me help you find your center through spirituality because spirituality is based on your emotional health.

Both spirituality and emotional health are about seeking peace of mind and a sense of purpose, where acceptance, gratitude, and a positive outlook on life are the outcome. Spirituality can help you find a connection between your mind and body to begin the healing process, which can be based on any form of spirituality with which you are comfortable.

Gina Rodriguez a Star Under Pressure

Sometimes we say things we don't mean but are allowed to take it back or let slide. When you are a celebrity, words you say are recorded and chronicled to be dredged up when the need arises.

Puerto Rican actress Gina Rodriguez confesses to breaking down and drowning in her anxiety as her statements on salaries for people of color were scrutinized and analyzed. She admits to dealing with anxiety but finds the constant judgment too much. She broke down in tears at one point during an interview where she was again asked to clarify her statement that was perceived as being against people of color (Betancourt, 2019). The stress and anxiety were aggravated to a level that became unbearable.

Finding strength and confidence in yourself will help you to over-come your sensitivity toward outside perceptions of who you are and is necessary to overcome your stresses; finding your center and purpose can help. And tapping into spirituality is one of the best methods to do so.

On What Is Spirituality Based?

Many paths can help you find your center and connection between body and soul; spirituality can be found in religion, the belief that you are governed by a higher power, in prayer, and through holistic practices like yoga or meditation.

How Can Spirituality Help withAnxiety?

Let's look at how spirituality can help you manage your anxiety and improve your overall mental well-being.

- Find your center and purpose in life

Spirituality is about focusing on the positive. Belief, faith, gratitude, and awe must be combined to discover what is amazing about yourself, your situation, and your surroundings. Become aware, humble, accepting, and focused on all the positive aspects of your life; discover what is essential and what makes you happy. If religion is your spirituality, read the words of wisdom found in the Bible, Quran, or other manuscripts to see your situation differently while finding a higher purpose in life and shifting your focus from worrying about your anxiety toward a greater goal.

- Learn to bond and become part of something outside of yourself

Find your center and focus on your spirituality. Whether that is through religion, joining a community, indulging in art, or immersing yourself in the wonder of nature, you can find a way to bond and become a part of something greater than you. Shift your focus from your anxieties as you become immersed in what is happening around you, become involved and as you merge in and find where you belong, you will not have much time to dwell on your dark and negative thoughts.

- Learn to focus on hope

Spirituality is an excellent tool for learning to focus on the positive. Through meditation, you can learn to be present in the moment. By concentrating, you can find purpose and a way to block the negative voices and see hope even in the darkest situations.

- Strengthen your mind

You can learn to deal with your anxious thoughts and panic better by teaching your mind to become stronger. Learn to be calm and avoid overreacting when dealing with disturbing situations. By becoming more attuned to yourself and your perceptions, you become wiser in understanding problems and other people.

- Enjoy a sense of belonging

Most people who practice spirituality do so as a community that shares a tight bond. If religion is your spirituality, you will find your place of worship has a strong community that is also a support group to each other.

Using Spirituality to Conquer Anxiety

Whether you are religious or focus your spirituality on other aspects, here are activities to incorporate spirituality into your routine to combat your anxiety.

Talk or Pray

Talking is a therapeutic practice that helps you relieve anxiety. Prayer is how you speak to God. It is a therapeutic practice; through prayer, you can discuss your inhibitions, fears, and shortcomings. Give thanks for what you have and what you hope to achieve. When you talk through prayer, you establish a spiritual connection with a higher power that you believe can support you to change your life. Prayer is something that gets easier the more you do it. There are no rules to go by, just open your heart and your mind as you speak to God. God talks to you through scripture or the still small voice.

Talk can be non-religious too. Mirror talk is a therapeutic practice that helps you to hold a conversation with yourself. Talk to your image as though you are a fan. Tell yourself how amazing you are, just as you are, and there is no need to strive for perfection.

Practice Loving-Kindness Meditation

Sit in a quiet spot and then self-reflect. Repeat three or four phrases that tell you how wonderful you are and what a great job you are doing. Instill confidence and love for yourself. Alternatively, you can think about a kindness someone did for you. Let the warmth of gratitude wash over you, and embrace it. Feel loved and appreciated.

Create a Harmonious Environment in Your Home

Make your home a spiritual place. Open the blinds, light incense sticks or scented candles, and play either spiritual songs of praise or soothing music. Clean up the clutter and free space in your home to let in good vibes, which will, in turn, clear your mind.

Incorporate Spirituality into Your Schedule

Avoid procrastination and add focus and meaning to your life by establishing a timetable to follow your spirituality. If you work from home or are a busy mom, set aside time for connecting with your spirituality.

- Time to reflect and pray

- Meditate

- Add in a morning run or walk

- Take time to relax and read scripture or an uplifting book

Imagine

Through imagination, you can reach many places and indulge in activities otherwise out of your reach. Find a spot to sit quietly, close your eyes, and imagine yourself someplace relaxing—a sunny beach in the Maldives, a meadow filled with wildflowers, and a snow-capped mountain. Next, focus on what you are doing—swimming with dolphins, laying on soft grass, or snowboarding down the slopes. Imagine the thrill you would feel and encourage the emotions. Virtual escapades are scientifically proven to reduce stress levels and were found to be helpful during the COVID-19 isolation period (Zamani et al., 2019).

Imagination can even come in the form of religion. Take the Bible, for example; you can choose to read a verse, then close your eyes and reflect on the words. Imagine yourself conquering your anxiety using the words and wisdom listed in the verses. Practice this with any teaching from any religion using imagination and meditation.

Spirituality and Your Relationship

Praying together creates a stronger bond between partners and families. Children who accompany their parents to worship in their church/mosque/synagogue, etc., find deeper meaning in spirituality and inner peace.

Spirituality introduces peace and stability to a home, marriage, or union. Following the teachings of religion helps a family or couple to stay grounded. Even non-religious spiritual practices will help bring clarity and a sense of respect when you both learn to focus, appreciate, and see each other in awe.

Cognitive behavioral therapy is similar to spirituality, as it helps people with serious anxiety issues to express themselves openly. Learn about arming yourself with the skills of DBT therapy next.

CHAPTER 9

— • —

NINE DBT TECHNIQUES TO REDUCE ANXIETY

C‍*an't you see, a spilled glass of milk to you can seem like an earthquake to me.* —Tiffaney L Ganci (Ganci, 2018)

You learned about cognitive behavioral therapy (CBT), and now let's learn about dialectical behavioral therapy (DBT). Learn to control your thoughts and behavior and live in the moment without external stresses influencing your present mood and reactions. DBT techniques will teach you self-regulation to better cope with stress.

Jennifer Lopez, a Star Who Needed Help Coping with Panic Attacks

Our final muse is Jennifer Lopez, a superstar and a person with ordinary feelings like you and me. Jennifer talks about the panic and anxiety that started to build up once her fame increased with the movie Selena. She admits to freaking out when strangers approached her on the streets, and she acknowledges that she has not been out alone now for the last 20 years.

Jennifer, who did not know how to acknowledge her anxiety, faced several panic attacks over time. The most significant one came when she realized it was time to divorce her then-husband Marc Anthony (Ngo, 2022).

Realizations that shock and sadden us make our thoughts and behavior erratic and getting those runaway emotions on track is what DBT techniques aim to teach you.

What Is DBT?

Dialectical behavioral therapy helps people deal with violent or self-destructive behavior. Intended to treat personality disorders, DBT has become an evidence-based therapy with a high success rate in people acquiring distress tolerance skills.

What Are Distress Tolerance Skills?

Your ability to manage your distress through thoughts, emotions, and behavior in response to a stressful situation is described as distress tolerance. DBT can help you acquire distress tolerance skills through techniques that teach self-soothing, shifting negative thoughts through distraction, and focusing on pros and cons.

DBT/Distress Tolerance Techniques

One Mindfully

It teaches you to focus on the task and looks at multitasking as unsuccessful and stressful. One mindfully asks that you focus on the task at hand. If you worry about your exam, you worry about that particular exam and not about past or future exam marks—it only increases the load of rumination worry.

One mindfully should be applied to every aspect of your life; washing the dishes, walking the dog, driving to work, grocery shopping, etc.

How much of your daily worry and anxiety is from the past and the future? Always live your life in the present and reduce your load of stress and worry.

TIPP

Here are the methods and how you can use the TIPP technique to calm down.

T=cool down your elevated temperature; splash cool water on your face; go for a walk if it's chilly outside or take a quick shower. However, do not overdo the chill factor.

I=intense exercise for 10–15 minutes will help you to work through the built-up energy/anger and tension. A brisk walk, run, or even jumping jacks will work.

P=paced breathing can help when tension and stress increase your heart rate and cause excessive sweating and dry mouth. Practice belly breathing, as I have explained in chapter 5.

P=progressive muscle relaxation. Sit with your back straight. Become aware of your upper back and tense your muscles; hold for five seconds and relax. Repeat all over your body, your lower back, arms, abdomen, buttocks, thighs, calves, and upper leg.

ACCEPTS

ACCEPTS is an acronym for a series of activities and thoughts that help you to focus and distract your mind from wandering or dwelling on anxiety.

A=Activities you focus on entirely when going for a walk, cleaning your home, playing a board game with your kids, sitting in at an office meeting.

C=Contributions to make yourself feel good. Donate stuff you no longer use, call a friend to see how they are, visit a sick relative, or volunteer at your local shelter.

C=Comparisons help you compare yourself and your situation. Start with how you are feeling at present, as opposed to how you felt before, and think about others not so lucky as you are dealing with similar issues. Read about people in dire situations and think about how lucky and blessed you are.

E=Emotions can be experimented on to stop yourself from becoming numb and focusing on just one aspect of your anxiety. Watch a romantic but sad movie, read books with varied endings, watch a comedy that has you rolling on the floor, or a horror show that gives you goosebumps. Listen to soothing music, religious songs that inspire, and music that motivates and makes you want to achieve your goals.

P=Pushing away. Refuse to entertain your negative thoughts. Push them aside and do not dwell on them. Say no to your negativity and put your major worries in the cupboard for a day and lock them up.

T=Thoughts that distract are good to keep rumination worry at bay. Count—anything; the number of trees on your street—the raindrops on your window, the cars parked outside your home. Perhaps work a puzzle or sing a song over and over in your head, trying to get the lyrics right.

S=Sensations. A great distraction is to feed your sensations. Hold a piece of ice to your face or in your hand. Take a cold shower, play in the snow, or listen to loud music.

Improve Skills

Replace the unpleasant moment with a thought or action that improves and makes it bearable.

- Use imagery to transport yourself from an unpleasant situation to one you can tolerate. A beach in the tropics, or even your favorite chair at home, where you relax and feel safe.

- Add meaning to your day, find a purpose for your actions, and improve on that negative feeling.

- Pray and find inner peace and a deeper, wiser understanding as you leave your worries in the care of a higher power.

- Relaxation techniques can help improve the moment. Meditation, deep breathing, a massage, or a hot bath.

- One mindfully can help you find the positive in that situation and place your complete focus there.

- Vacation. Take a break and let out your inner child. Explore the woods in your backyard, let nature wow you, go for a swim, or spend the day at the lake/beach.

- Encouragement. Practice self-motivation and praise yourself and your efforts.

Self-Soothing

Learn to relax by influencing your five senses: touch, taste, smell, sight, and hearing. Diffuse a distressing situation by using one of your five senses to distract yourself. Choose the stimulus that works for you.

Sight—you may like looking at beautiful scenery/pictures/movies.

Sound—listen to your favorite music, your children's laughter as they play, play a soothing track, or listen to an audiobook/podcast.

Smell—dab on your favorite perfume, bake something, use lightly scented candles or incense sticks, smell your baby's head, and hug your partner's pillow.

Taste—eat something you like chewing slowly and savoring each mouthful, drink tea or coffee, and have a fruit/sweet.

Touch—pet your cat or dog and stroke their fur, go for a massage, and feel something velvety soft like a cushion.

Pros and Cons

In DBT, looking at the pros and cons encourages you to take both roads. The pros and cons of acting on your impulsive mood and the pros and cons of not acting on your impulsive mood. It gives you a chance to debate every angle instead of just looking at the pros and cons of not acting on your impulse. Looking at every angle allows you to make a good and more accurate decision because you have covered every angle.

Let's say your friend says something to hurt you that reminds you of a past incident. You wonder about calling her out on it, letting it slide, and then dealing with your destructive emotions on your own.

You could acknowledge it and then have it out with your friend, who probably had no bad intentions at the start. You could also go home and try to understand why she said it and how you can ride it out without causing damage to your relationship or your emotional state.

Debate the pros and cons from both angles and then come to the wisest decision, which you will know is the correct one by instinct.

DEAR MAN

This DBT skill will help you form healthy relationships with others, ascertain yourself, and build self-confidence.

D=describe what you are going through and why, so the person understands the reason for your distress.

E=express and let the other person know your feelings and emotions without assuming they already know.

A=assert yourself, don't be afraid or shy. Say "no" if you must.

R=reinforce your reasoning and the positive side of providing you with your needs. You could also tell them what to expect if your needs are unmet.

M=mindful. Stay focused on your demands and needs. Do not get intimidated. If needed, repeat your requests, and let the other person know you are not ready to back down. Ignore all distractions, especially any form of verbal attack.

A=appear. Project yourself as confident and capable. Use your actions and tone of voice to ascertain yourself. Avoid looking meek; do not stutter, look down, or seem nervous.

N=negotiate and be open to suggestions that will help you to get what you need. You can refuse suggestions only after weighing the pros and cons of what is offered.

Radical Acceptance

Accepting facts as reality and saving yourself the heartache of prolonged pain brought on by a situation is radical acceptance. Understanding factors beyond your control will help you become accepting of a situation. Here are ten steps to achieve radical acceptance.

1. Acknowledge you are questioning the reality of a situation.

2. Tell yourself there are reasons for that reality.

3. Face the reality of the situation and remind yourself of what you cannot control or change.

4. Accept the situation you cannot control with your mind, body, and soul. Do so with self-talk, imagery, or mindful meditation.

5. Make a list of how you would face the situation if you accepted the reality of it. Then proceed to follow through on how you would behave if you encountered the situation.

6. Imagine what would happen if you accepted the situation and what it would be like if you did not.

7. Become aware of how your body reacts to your acceptance of the situation.

8. Let grief and sadness invade your being. Feel the emotions.

9. Accept that even through the pain, you can still find a purpose for living.

10. Make a list of the pros and cons if you feel you will need help to accept the situation.

Opposite Action

DBT uses opposite actions to make you do the opposite of what your emotions are asking you to do. This is because a heightened stage of emotional behavior makes you do things you haven't thought through; hence, if your initial reaction is to scream and throw a tantrum, do the opposite and quietly walk away.

This action doesn't warrant ignoring your emotions; instead, it's seen as choosing a healthier option. Instead of moaning about a lost relationship and isolating yourself at home, you would go out with friends—the opposite here is less harmful than the initial reaction.

Opposite action takes practice, though, and you must make conscious efforts to make it happen. But as with everything else, the action becomes an automatic reflex with practice.

Each technique listed here will help you overcome your anxieties and panic attacks at different points. They are a combination of techniques I have addressed throughout the book. By being aware and mindful, you will find success and control over your thoughts, mind, and behavior.

Chapter 10

Anxiety Journal Guide

The proven benefits of journaling toward anxiety are invaluable and offer you a range of benefits. Writing about past trauma in your journal and shifting it out of your mind will help you to accept the emotion and the hurt associated with the incident. Journaling can help you to look at problems from a different perspective and actively evaluate your thoughts, feelings, and behavior.

The prompts and the activities listed here will help you to get started. Cultivating the habit of journaling and focusing more on your anxieties is a way to find a solution.

Worksheet 1: Identify Yourself and Your Anxieties

Here is a list of prompts to help you identify your anxieties, triggers, and stresses. Use this page at the end of your day as a guide to explore your emotions and experiences. Take one prompt daily, enter it in your focus journal, and add your thoughts to answer the question. In the end, step back and look at what you have written, and you may discover more about yourself than you thought you knew.

The most difficult experience I faced so far was when...

- I feel most anxious or panicked when faced with... List three things.

- What emotions did you experience today? Why? and what was the reason? Think about your initial reaction; what are the pros and cons of it?

- Today and for the next three days, you must choose three people closest to you and write them letters. Include your thoughts, fears, gratitude, and any issues you may have with them. You don't have to post them; keep them to read for yourself. (Your parents/partner/friend/boss)

- What are you the proudest of achieving so far?

- Who has complimented you ever? What were they?

- List ten moments in your life when you felt happy and content; even childhood memories count—

- Who has hurt you the most? Can you forgive them? What would you say?

- I had my first panic attack when I was... How did it make you feel? Is that reason still a trigger?

Worksheet 2: Evaluate Your Anxiety—Can You Turn It Around?

To learn more about your anxiety, use the questions in this worksheet to conclude positively about your worries and stresses.

How bad would you rate your anxiety on a scale of one to ten (1=mild, 10=severe)

Explain the reason behind your score. Read it again

Now, re-evaluate your score. Do you have the capacity to add more control to your anxiety?

How would you like to feel when you wake up in the morning?

1. Is there an adjustment you would like to make to your routine in the morning?

2. What scares me?... Why is that?... Can I control it?...

3. List three reasons why you think you are too tough on yourself... Can you change that perception?...

4. List three instances your general worry helped you. (You finished your project at work on time/your kids scored well at exams because you stressed over their studies and helped them/any other reasons you can come up with)

5. When anxiety takes over your thoughts, how does your behavior change?... Can you control it?...

6. What are the stresses you feel you can control?...

7. If I were to describe myself, I would say I am...

8. My superpower is... (list your strengths) one for each day of the week, and then try to focus on that superpower throughout that day.

Example: Monday—I can practice deep breathing to calm down

Worksheet 3: Conquer Overthinking

Here's what you are going to do to conquer your overthinking. Choose a time each day to worry. You can only permit yourself to worry excessively during that time of the day. Choose a time when you are alone and free. Perhaps it is after the kids have left for school, after work, once you are home and settled down, any time that gives you a half hour to worry uninterrupted. Until that time, be mindful and let those little worries that pop into your head pass by. Do not entertain them. If you like, have a little notebook to jot down the concerns to take up later during your worry time.

My Worry Schedule

Choose a time frame—20 to 30 minutes is best.

- Choose the place and time—make sure it's a private and uncomfortable spot you will not want to settle into. It should be a spot you view with distaste, and in time you will view worry similarly.

- Go through your worries individually and use the DBT techniques. Think about the severity of the worry and how you can handle it.

- Apart from listing your worries, you can choose this time to work on your emotional triggers. Call a parent you avoid, assess your self-worth with them, write about a traumatic event, and practice deep breathing to calm yourself and learn to take control. Watch a video of a phobia to see how much panic you can learn to control and deflate that fear.

- Decide on an action to stop your worry time. Once you get into your worry cycle, stop after the allocated 20–30 minutes, do not exceed. Set the alarm and choose an action that will help you switch activities. Turning on the television, getting lunch or dinner started, etc.

Worksheet 4: Processing My Trauma Trigger—My Thoughts, Emotions, and Actions

This very special worksheet is to be used when you have experienced a sudden emotional trigger and feel the need to analyze the trauma and come to terms with it.

- The incident – the trigger, write about what happened.

Write a detailed description starting with events that led up to the final episode. Spare no detail. List everything done and said, as well as who said what and who did what. Make this recollection as precise as possible and keep it as a reference for future panic attacks based on this trigger. The more you analyze it, the less impact it will have on you.

I feel... (list every emotion you are feeling. Hurt, anger, disappointment, fear, sadness). Sometimes you may feel both sad and angry at the same time, and that is quite alright. Analyze the situation and see why you have conflicting emotions.

- Connect this trigger to your trauma. Reflect on the incident, re-read your account, and see where you can identify the events that triggered your panic attack. It may be a word, an action, or anything else. Ask yourself why that trigger reminded you of your trauma.

- My coping system.

How did you cope? Or are you trying to cope now?

What method are you using, and is it working?

What can you do to prevent future attacks from taking place?

Can you break down the trigger to see how you are most affected?

Journaling is only an aid to help you look deeper into yourself; it is not a remedy for continuous anxiety or panic. If you cannot control your emotions and negative talk, it is best to seek help from a professional.

— • —

CONCLUSION

D iscovering your anxieties are approachable and that you can tackle them is a start to a new you. Make a resolve to conquer your fear, worry, and panic—looking forward to healthier, happier, and more fulfilling relationships.

Anxiety is real and needs to be acknowledged, but you are in control and have always been. You have now been armed with the tools to fight back. Use the techniques in my book to successfully conquer your anxieties and finally live a life free from the burden of panic attacks and uncontrollable thoughts—remember, you are stronger than you think you are!

This book is also available on Amazon and Audible. If you enjoyed this book and found it helpful, please leave a review.

REFERENCES

10 Surprisingly Common Anxiety Triggers : Intrepid Mental Wellness, PLLC: Psychiatric Nurse Practitioners. (n.d.). Www.intrep idmentalhealth.com. https://www.intrepidmentalhealth.com/blo g/10-surprisingly-common-anxiety-triggers

Abraham, M. (2020, October). *Emotional Abuse and Anxiety*. Www. calmclinic.com. https://www.calmclinic.com/anxiety/causes/emo tional-abuse

Abuse, trauma, and mental health. (2018, August 28). Womenshe alth.gov. https://www.womenshealth.gov/mental-health/abuse-t rauma-and-mental-health

Al Sunni, A., & Latif, R. (2014). Effects of chocolate intake on Per- ceived Stress; a Controlled Clinical Study. *International Journal of Health Sciences, 8*(4), 393–401. https://www.ncbi.nlm.nih.gov/pm c/articles/PMC4350893/

American Psychiatric Association. (2019, January). *Psychiatry.org - What is Psychotherapy?* Psychiatry.org. https://psychiatry.org/pati ents-families/psychotherapy

Amsterdam, J. D., Li, Q. S., Xie, S. X., & Mao, J. J. (2019). Putative Antidepressant Effect of Chamomile (Matricaria chamomilla L.) Oral Extract in Subjects with Comorbid Generalized Anxiety Disor- der and Depression. *The Journal of Alternative and Complementary Medicine*. https://doi.org/10.1089/acm.2019.0252

Anderson, E., & Shivakumar, G. (2013). Effects of Exercise and Physical Activity on Anxiety. *Frontiers in Psychiatry*, 4(27). https://doi.org/10.3389/fpsyt.2013.00027

Andriota, M. (2022, March 10). *Breathing In Sync: Intimacy Building Exercises and Benefits*. Psych Central. https://psychcentral.com/lib/mindfulness-in-relationships-breathing-together#benefits

Anxiety and Depression Association of America. (2021, April 21). *Facts & statistics*. ADAA. https://adaa.org/understanding-anxiety/facts-statistics

Anxiety Canada – MAPS. (n.d.). Anxiety Canada - MAPS. https://maps.anxietycanada.com/courses/anxiety-plan-for-adults/

Anxiety UK. (2017, December 19). *5 ways swimming can boost your mental health (guest blog)*. Anxiety UK. https://www.anxietyuk.org.uk/blog/5-ways-regular-swimming-can-boost-mental-health-guest-blog/#:~:text=Lower%20anxiety%20and%20depression

Anxiety: 5 Signs That It's a Problem for You. (2018, January 17). Health Essentials from Cleveland Clinic. https://health.clevelandclinic.org/anxiety-5-signs-that-its-a-problem-for-you/

Aquin, J. P., El-Gabalawy, R., Sala, T., & Sareen, J. (2017). Anxiety Disorders and General Medical Conditions: Current Research and Future Directions. *Focus (American Psychiatric Publishing)*, 15(2), 173–181. https://doi.org/10.1176/appi.focus.20160044

Arachnophobia (Fear of Spiders): Overview & Treatment. (n.d.). Cleveland Clinic. https://my.clevelandclinic.org/health/diseases/21852-arachnophobia-fear-of-spiders

Aslam, S. (2020, November 15). *3 Simple Ways to Embrace Your Anxiety*. Invisible Illness. https://medium.com/invisible-illness/3-simple-ways-to-embrace-your-anxiety-6cd9813b9395

Azami, M., Shohani, M., Badfar, G., Nasirkandy, M., Kaikhavani, S., Rahmati, S., Modmeli, Y., & Soleymani, A. (2018). The effect of yoga on stress, anxiety, and depression in women. *International Journal of Preventive Medicine*, *9*(1), 21. https://doi.org/10.4103/ijpvm.ijpvm_242_16

Bartels, H., Middel, B. L., van der Laan, B. F. A. M., Staal, M. J., & Albers, F. W. J. (2008). The Additive Effect of Co-Occurring Anxiety and Depression on Health Status, Quality of Life and Coping Strategies in Help-Seeking Tinnitus Sufferers. *Ear and Hearing*, *29*(6), 947–956. https://doi.org/10.1097/aud.0b013e3181888f83

Bauer, M., Heinz, A., & Whybrow, P. C. (2002). Thyroid hormones, serotonin and mood: of synergy and significance in the adult brain. *Molecular Psychiatry*, *7*(2), 140–156. https://doi.org/10.1038/sj.mp.4000963

Berger, P., Bitsch, F., & Falkenberg, I. (2021). Humor in Psychiatry: Lessons From Neuroscience, Psychopathology, and Treatment Research. *Frontiers in Psychiatry*, *12*. https://doi.org/10.3389/fpsyt.2021.681903

Betancourt, B. (2019, June 19). *43 Spiritual Ways To Manage Stress, Anxiety & Depression*. Https://Mattbeech.com/. https://mattbeech.com/spiritual-ways-manage-stress-anxiety-depression/

Beyond Blue. (2019). *What causes anxiety*. Beyondblue.org.au; beyondblue. https://www.beyondblue.org.au/the-facts/anxiety/what-causes-anxiety

Boyle, N., Lawton, C., & Dye, L. (2017). The Effects of Magnesium Supplementation on Subjective Anxiety and Stress—A Systematic Review. *Nutrients, 9*(5), 429. https://doi.org/10.3390/nu9050429

Bräuninger, Ph.D., I. (2015, March 6). *Dance Therapy Can Alleviate Anxiety.* Anxiety.org. https://www.anxiety.org/what-is-dance-movement-therapy

Brett, W. (2015, April 21). *Anxiety and Social Exclusion.* Will Bratt C o u n s e l l i n g . https://www.willbrattcounselling.com/blog-creating-difference/2015/4/18/anxiety-social-exclusion#:~:text=The%20concept%20of%20social%20exclusion

British Cycling. (n.d.). *5 ways cycling can help improve your mental health.* British Cycling. Retrieved September 3, 2022, from https://www.britishcycling.org.uk/about/article/5-ways-cycling-can-help-improve-your-mental-health#:~:text=A%20study%20in%20Science%20Direct

C Steuart, C. (2022, April 12). *9 foods that help reduce anxiety.* Www.medicalnewstoday.com. https://www.medicalnewstoday.com/articles/322652#foods-that-help-reduce-anxiety

Casie, A. J. (2020, August 28). *10 Tips To Start The Day On A Postive Note.* GenTwenty. https://gentwenty.com/start-the-day-on-a-positive-note/

Cassata, C. (2021, December 2). *The Evidence Is Adding Up: What You Eat Can Directly Impact Stress and Anxiety.* Verywell Mind. https://www.verywellmind.com/what-you-eat-can-have-an-effect-on-your-overall-mental-well-being-5209290

Catanese, N. (2013, July 31). *How Diet Affects Relationships — Food, Romantic Mood.* Www.refinery29.com. https://www.refinery29.com/en-us/2013/07/50802/diet-affects-relationships

Causes - Agoraphobia. (2021, February 12). Nhs.uk. https://www.n hs.uk/mental-health/conditions/agoraphobia/causes/

Chan, A. (2021, May 3). *Ariana Grande Encourages Ending Stigma Surrounding Mental Health: "The Work Is So Hard."* Billboard. https://www.billboard.com/music/music-news/ariana-gra nde-encourages-ending-mental-health-stigma-9566721/

Cleveland Clinic. (2019). *Diaphragmatic Breathing Exercises & Techniques | Cleveland Clinic*. Cleveland Clinic. https://my.clevelandcli nic.org/health/articles/9445-diaphragmatic-breathing

Clinic, M. (n.d.). *7 great reasons why exercise matters*. Mayo Clinic. https://www.mayoclinic.org/healthy-lifestyle/fitness/in-depth/exe rcise/art-20048389#:~:text=Exercise%20boosts%20energy&text= Regular%20physical%20activity%20can%20improve

Coplan, J. D., Hodulik, S., Mathew, S. J., Mao, X., Hof, P. R., Gorman, J. M., & Shungu, D. C. (2012). The Relationship between Intelligence and Anxiety: An Association with Subcortical White Matter Metabolism. *Frontiers in Evolutionary Neuroscience, 3*. https://doi.org/10 .3389/fnevo.2011.00008

Cuncic, A. (2018). *What Does It Mean to Be "Triggered?"* Verywell Mind. https://www.verywellmind.com/what-does-it-mean-to -be-triggered-4175432

Dawn, R. (2018, May 16). *Selma Blair opens up about her anxiety and depression in heartfelt post*. TODAY.com . https://www.today.com/popculture/selma-blair-opens-about-h er-anxiety-depression-heartfelt-post-t129144

DBT. (n.d.-a). *DBT : TIPP - Skills, Worksheets, Videos, & Activities*. DBT. https://dialecticalbehaviortherapy.com/distress-tolerance/tipp/

DBT. (n.d.-b). *Pros and Cons*. DBT Self Help. https://dbtselfhelp.co m/dbt-skills-list/distress-tolerance/pros-and-cons/

DBT. (n.d.-c). *Self Soothing*. DBT. https://dialecticalbehaviortherap y.com/distress-tolerance/self-soothing/

Delagran, L. (n.d.). *What Is Spirituality?* Taking Charge of Your Health & Wellbeing. https://www.takingcharge.csh.umn.edu/what-spirituality#:~: text=Spirituality%20is%20a%20broad%20concept

Digital Communications Division (DCD). (2015, August 21). *What are the five major types of anxiety disorders?* HHS.gov. https://www.hhs.gov/answers/mental-health-and-substance-abu se/what-are-the-five-major-types-of-anxiety-disorders/index.htm l

DiNicolantonio, J. J., & O'Keefe, J. H. (2018). Omega-6 vegetable oils as a driver of coronary heart disease: the oxidized linoleic acid hypothesis. *Open Heart*, *5*(2), e000898. https://doi.org/10.1136/o penhrt-2018-000898

doctor.ndtv.com. (2008, July 5). *If You Have These Personality Traits, You Are Most Likely To Suffer From Anxiety*. Doctor.ndtv.co m. https://doctor.ndtv.com/living-healthy/personality-traits-linke d-to-anxiety-disorders-1878210

Eagleson, C., Hayes, S., Mathews, A., Perman, G., & Hirsch, C. R. (2016). The power of positive thinking: Pathological worry is reduced by thought replacement in Generalized Anxiety Disorder. *Behaviour Research and Therapy*, *78*, 13–18. https://doi.org/10.10 16/j.brat.2015.12.017

Eisold, K. (2021). *How to become friends with your anxiety: You Are Not Alone mental health series with 3News' Hollie Strano*. Wkyc.com. https://www.wkyc.com/article/news/health/mental-health/anxiet

y-advice-wendy-suzuki-book-good-anxiety-harnessing-the-power -of-the-most-misunderstood-emotion/95-f3a3f63f-9762-404b-a2 76-f230293ed6d6

Erickson, K. I., Voss, M. W., Prakash, R. S., Basak, C., Szabo, A., Chaddock, L., Kim, J. S., Heo, S., Alves, H., White, S. M., Wojcicki, T. R., Mailey, E., Vieira, V. J., Martin, S. A., Pence, B. D., Woods, J. A., McAuley, E., & Kramer, A. F. (2011). Exercise training increases size of hippocampus and improves memory. *Proceedings of the National Academy of Sciences, 108*(7), 3017–3022. https://doi.org /10.1073/pnas.1015950108

Family Stress | SCAN Families. (2013, September 5). Family Programs. https://scanfamilies.org/resource/family-stress/

Fernandez, A. R. M. (2017, September 29). *Separation Anxiety in Adults: Symptoms, Treatment, and More*. Healthline. https://www.healthline.com/health/separation-anxiety-in-a dults#:~:text=Separation%20anxiety%20isn

Fltetcher, J. (2019, February 12). *4-7-8 breathing: How it works, benefits, and uses*. Www.medicalnewstoday.com. https://www.medic alnewstoday.com/articles/324417#how-to-do-it

Fusar-Poli, L., Vozza, L., Gabbiadini, A., Vanella, A., Concas, I., Tinacci, S., Petralia, A., Signorelli, M. S., & Aguglia, E. (2019). Curcumin for depression: a meta-analysis. *Critical Reviews in Food Science and Nutrition*, 1–11. https://doi.org/10.1080/10408398.2019.1653260

Ganci, T. L. (2018, April). *Living With Anxiety, Breathe, Teen Mental Illness Poem*. Family Friend Poems. https://www.familyfriendpoe ms.com/poem/breathe-7

Generalized Anxiety Disorder (GAD) | Anxiety and Depression Association of America, ADAA. (n.d.). Adaa.org. https://adaa.org/understanding-anxiety/generalized-anxiety-diso

rder-gad#:~:text=Generalized%20Anxiety%20Disorder%20(GAD)
%20is

Gomez, J. (2019, April 19). *9 Times Ariana Grande Has Opened Up About Her Mental Health*. Seventeen; Seventeen. https://www.seventeen.com/celebrity/music/a27207297/ariana-grande-mental-health-anxiety/

Gomstyn, A. (2019). *Food for Your Mood: How What You Eat Affects Your Mental Health*. Aetna; Aetna. https://www.aetna.com/health-guide/food-affects-mental-health.html

Gonsalves, K. (2019, March 28). *The 3 Biggest Causes Of Stress In Relationships (And How To Handle It)*. Mindbodygreen. https://www.mindbodygreen.com/articles/the-3-biggest-causes-of-stress-in-relationships-and-how-to-handle-them

Harper, B. (2021, April 12). *Amanda Seyfried opens up about panic attacks: "It feels like life or death."* Www.yahoo.com . https://www.yahoo.com/lifestyle/amanda-seyfried-panic-attacks-mental-health-220717301.html

Harris, A. (2022, June 8). *#stayhomestayhopeful - Radical Acceptance in a Time of Uncertainty*. Hopeway.org. https://hopeway.org/blog/radical-acceptance

Higgins, L. (2021, May 9). *Cognitive Reframing: Overcoming Cognitive Distortions with Reframing*. The Couch: A Therapy & Mental Wellness Blog. https://blog.zencare.co/cognitive-reframing-distortions/

Holland, M. (2022a, February 24). *15 Common Anxiety Triggers & How to Cope With Them*. Choosing Therapy. https://www.choosingtherapy.com/anxiety-triggers/

Holland, M. (2022b, July 20). *Why Does My Mom Hate Me? Why You May Feel This Way & What to Do.* Choosing Therapy. https://www.choosingtherapy.com/why-does-my-mom-hate-me/

Hurst, K. (2014, September 15). *Why Positive Thinkers Have Better Relationships.* The Law of Attraction. https://thelawofattraction.com/why-positive-thinkers-have-better-relationships/

Jiannine, L. (2018). An investigation of the relationship between physical fitness, self-concept, and sexual functioning. *Journal of Education and Health Promotion, 7*(1), 57. https://doi.org/10.4103/jehp.jehp_157_17

Centers for Disease Control and Prevention. (1999). Stress at work. *The National Institute for Occupational Safety and Health.* pub99101

Joy, R. (2018, November 29). *Automatic Negative Thinking: 5 Ways to Stop These Invading Thoughts.* Healthline. https://www.healthline.com/health/mental-health/stop-automatic-negative-thoughts#2-recognize-automatic-negative-thinking

Klynn, B. (2021, June 22). *Emotional regulation: Skills, exercises, and strategies.* Www.betterup.com. https://www.betterup.com/blog/emotional-regulation-skills

Knight, L. K., Stoica, T., Depue, B. E., & Fogelman, N. D. (2019, March 19). *Convergent Neural Correlates of Empathy and Anxiety During Socioemotional Processing.* https://www.frontiersin.org/articles/10.3389/fnhum.2019.00094/full

Lear, S. (2020, February 10). *Exercise your way to a better relationship.* The Conversation. https://theconversation.com/exercise-your-way-to-a-better-relationship-131172#:~:text=Exercise%20has%20a%20lot%20of

Lee, C. (2021, June 2). *Industrial Seed Oils Make You Anxious, Depressed, and Feisty*. Medium. https://catyleeee.medium.com/industrial-seed-oils-make-you-anxious-depressed-and-feisty-7af1476944e3

Lindseth, G. N., Coolahan, S. E., Petros, T. V., & Lindseth, P. D. (2014). Neurobehavioral Effects of Aspartame Consumption. *Research in Nursing & Health*, *37*(3), 185–193. https://doi.org/10.1002/nur.21595

Linehan, M. (n.d.). *DEAR MAN Skill*. Dialectical Behavior Therapy (DBT) Tools. https://dbt.tools/interpersonal_effectiveness/dear-man.php

Linehan, M. (2022a). *ACCEPTS Skill*. Dialectical Behavior Therapy (DBT) Tools. https://dbt.tools/distress_tolerance/accepts.php

Linehan, M. (2022b). *IMPROVE Skill*. Dialectical Behavior Therapy (DBT) Tools. https://dbt.tools/distress_tolerance/improve.php

Liu, L., & Zhu, G. (2018). Gut–Brain Axis and Mood Disorder. *Frontiers in Psychiatry*, *9*. https://doi.org/10.3389/fpsyt.2018.00223

Loewe, E. (2018, May 29). *The Simple Exercise That Could Help Calm Anxiety, According To Science*. Mindbodygreen. https://www.mindbodygreen.com/articles/why-walking-is-the-answer-to-anxiety

Lukas, E. (n.d.). *Stop Asking Missy Elliott When Her New Album Is Coming*. Nylon. Retrieved September 4, 2022, from https://www.nylon.com/articles/missy-elliott-billboard-cover

Mayo Clinic. (2017, August 29). *Social anxiety disorder (social phobia) - symptoms and causes*. Mayo Clinic; Mayo Clinic. https://www.mayoclinic.org/diseases-conditions/social-anxiety-disorder/symptoms-causes/syc-20353561

Mayo Clinic. (2018). *Anxiety disorders - symptoms and causes*. Mayo Clinic; Mayo Foundation for Medical Education and Research. https://www.mayoclinic.org/diseases-conditions/anxiety/symptoms-causes/syc-20350961

McCallum, K. (2021, April 12). *When Overthinking Becomes a Problem & What You Can Do About It*. Www.houstonmethodist.org. https://www.houstonmethodist.org/blog/articles/2021/apr/when-overthinking-becomes-a-problem-and-what-you-can-do-about-it/

McLaughlin, K. A., Behar, E., & Borkovec, T. D. (2008). Family history of psychological problems in generalized anxiety disorder. *Journal of Clinical Psychology, 64*(7), 905–918. https://doi.org/10.1002/jclp.20497

Meghan. (2021, July 9). *How Emma Stone Dealt with Anxiety and Panic Attacks*. FHE Health – Addiction & Mental Health Care. https://fherehab.com/learning/emma-stone-anxiety-panic

Mills, K. I. (2014). *Religion or Spirituality Has Positive Impact on Romantic/Marital Relationships, Child Development, Research Shows Parenting, Families, Relationships*. Apa.org. https://www.apa.org/news/press/releases/2014/12/religion-relationships

Mind. (2021). *Housing and mental health*. Www.mind.org.uk. https://www.mind.org.uk/information-support/guides-to-support-and-services/housing/housing-and-mental-health/

Mirjalili, F. (2021, January 20). *Demi Lovato Reveals How She Keeps Her Anxiety In Check*. TheThings. https://www.thethings.com/demi-lovato-reveals-how-she-keeps-her-anxiety-in-check/

Moore, K. (2020, January 24). *DBT Skill: One-Mindfully*. Balance & Potential Inc. https://balanceandpotential.com/dbt-skill-one-mindfully/#:~:text=One%2DMindfully%20involves%20being%20fully

MPH, S. C., MD. (2021, June 25). *How can you manage anxiety during pregnancy?* Harvard Health. https://www.health.harvard.edu/blog/how-can-you-manage-anxiety-during-pregnancy-202106252512

Nast, C. (2015, November 24). *Missy Elliott Opens Up About Battling Anxiety*. SELF. https://www.self.com/story/missy-elliott-opens-up-about-battling-anxiety

Nast, C. (2021, October 8). *Ten Minutes in a SoulCycle Closet With Unlikely Wellness Poster Boy Shawn Mendes*. GQ. https://www.gq.com/story/how-shawn-mendes-became-the-poster-boy-for-wellness-and-mental-health

Natacci, L., M. Marchioni, D., C. Goulart, A., Nunes, M., B. Moreno, A., O. Cardoso, L., Giatti, L., B. Molina, M., S. Santos, I., R. Brunoni, A., A. Lotufo, P., & M. Bensenor, I. (2018). Omega 3 Consumption and Anxiety Disorders: A Cross-Sectional Analysis of the Brazilian Longitudinal Study of Adult Health (ELSA-Brasil). *Nutrients, 10*(6), 663. https://doi.org/10.3390/nu10060663

National Institute on Drug Abuse. (2020, April). *Part 1: The connection between substance use disorders and mental illness*. National Institute on Drug Abuse. https://nida.nih.gov/publications/research-reports/common-comorbidities-substance-use-disorders/part-1-connection-between-substance-use-disorders-mental-illness

Ngo, S. (2022, January 4). *Jennifer Lopez Talks About Her Panic Attacks | HISPANIC Network Magazine*. Hispanic Network Magazine | a Hispanic News Source. https://hnmagazine.com/2022/01/jennifer-lopez-talks-panic-attacks/

NHS. (2018). *Overview - Generalised Anxiety Disorder in Adults*. Nhs.uk. https://www.nhs.uk/mental-health/conditions/generalised-anxiety-disorder/overview/

North Star Transitions. (n.d.). *How Spirituality Can Help With Anxiety | Northstar Transitions*. Www.northstartransitions.com. Retrieved September 4, 2022, from https://www.northstartransitions.com/post/how-spirituality-can -help-with-anxiety#:~:text=Spiritual%20practices%20like%20pray er%20or

Now, L. (2018, May 1). *Can Childhood Trauma Cause Anxiety?* Bridges to Recovery. https://www.bridgestorecovery.com/blog/can-childhood-trauma -cause-anxiety-whats-the-best-way-to-approach-treatment/#:~:te xt=It%20is%20true%20that%20childhood

ParentCo. (2017, March). *Are Anxious People Actually Smarter?* ParentCo. https://www.parent.com/blogs/conversations/anxious-pe ople-actually-smarter

Perera, F., Nolte, E. L. Roen, Wang, Y., Margolis, A. E., Calafat, A. M., Wang, S., Garcia, W., Hoepner, L. A., Peterson, B. S., Rauh, V., & Herbstman, J. (2016). Bisphenol A exposure and symptoms of anxiety and depression among inner city children at 10–12 years of age. *Environmental Research, 151*, 195–202. https://doi.org/10. 1016/j.envres.2016.07.028

Princing, M. (2018, June 4). *What Is Deep Breathing?* Right as Rain by UW Medicine. https://rightasrain.uwmedicine.org/mind/stress/why-deep-breat hing-makes-you-feel-so-chill#:~:text=Deep%20breathing%20can %20help%20lessen

PsychDB. (2021, February 26). *Other Specified Anxiety Disorder*. PsychDB. https://www.psychdb.com/anxiety/z-other-specified-anxie ty

Pugle, M. (2022, January 6). *Anxious or Anxiety Disorder? Here's How to Tell the Difference*. EverydayHealth.com

. https://www.everydayhealth.com/anxiety-disorders/are-you-ju st-feeling-anxious-or-do-you-have-an-anxiety-disorder/

Renter, E. (2015). *How Job Stress Might Be Killing You, and What You Can Do About It*. US News & World Report; U.S. News & World R   e   p   o   r   t   . https://health.usnews.com/health-news/health-wellness/articles/ 2015/06/15/how-job-stress-might-be-killing-you-and-what-you-ca n-do-about-it

Richmond, C. (2003, February 7). *What Is Panic Disorder?* Web-MD; WebMD. https://www.webmd.com/anxiety-panic/guide/me ntal-health-panic-disorder

Roll, N. (2019, February 6). *Square Breathing: How to Reduce Stress through Breathwork | Zencare*. The Couch: A Therapy & Mental Wellness Blog. https://blog.zencare.co/square-breathing/

Safari, M. A., Koushkie Jahromi, M., Rezaei, R., Aligholi, H., & Brand, S. (2020). The Effect of Swimming on Anxiety-Like Behaviors and Corticosterone in Stressed and Unstressed Rats. *International Journal of Environmental Research and Public Health*, *17*(18), 6675. https://doi.org/10.3390/ijerph17186675

Schimelpfening, N. (2021, November 5). *What to Know About Di-alectical Behavior Therapy*. Verywell Mind. https://www.verywellm ind.com/dialectical-behavior-therapy-1067402

Scott, E. (2018). *How to Reduce Negative Self-Talk for a Better Life*. Verywell Mind. https://www.verywellmind.com/negative-self-talk -and-how-it-affects-us-4161304

Services, D. of H. & H. (2015). *Breathing to reduce stress*. Www.b etterhealth.vic.gov.au. https://www.betterhealth.vic.gov.au/healt h/healthyliving/breathing-to-reduce-stress

Sherri Gordon. (2019). *Bullying Can Lead to Anxiety Disorders*. Very-well Family. https://www.verywellfamily.com/bullying-and-anxiety-connection-460631

Silva Casabianca, S. (2021, May 6). *15 Cognitive Distortions to Blame for Your Negative Thinking*. Psych Central. https://psychcentral.com/lib/cognitive-distortions-negative-thinking#catastrophizing

Simopoulos, A. P. (2006). Evolutionary aspects of diet, the omega-6/omega-3 ratio and genetic variation: nutritional implications for chronic diseases. *Biomedicine & Pharmacotherapy, 60*(9), 502–507. https://doi.org/10.1016/j.biopha.2006.07.080

Smith, J. (2013, April 5). *Research Puts Focus on Positive Thinking in Relationships*. GoodTherapy.org Therapy Blog. https://www.goodtherapy.org/blog/relationships-positive-thinking-focus-0405137#:~:text=It%20has%20been%20said%20that

Smith, J., Telford*, R., Mason, I., & Weidemann, M. (1990). Exercise, Training and Neutrophil Microbicidal Activity. *International Journal of Sports Medicine, 11*(03), 179–187. https://doi.org/10.1055/s-2007-1024788

Smith, K. (2019, September 6). *Grief and Anxiety*. Www.psycom.net. https://www.psycom.net/anxiety-complicated-grief

Smith, M., Segal, R., & Segal, J. (2018). *Therapy for Anxiety Disorders: Cognitive Behavioral Therapy (CBT), Exposure Therapy, and Other Anxiety Treatments*. Helpguide.org. https://www.helpguide.org/articles/anxiety/therapy-for-anxiety-disorders.htm

Soul, T. R. (2020, January 24). *Psychology Explains Why You Need to Stop Avoiding Your Triggers*. Medium. https://therewiredsoul.medium.com/psychology-explains-why-you-need-to-stop-avoiding-your-triggers-ceb5c2147580

Sparks, D. (2019, May). *Mayo Mindfulness: Overcoming negative self-talk.* Https://Newsnetwork.mayoclinic.org/ . https://newsnetwork.mayoclinic.org/discussion/mayo-mindfulness-overcoming-negative-self-talk/

Stern Vitamin. (n.d.). *The role of micronutrients in mental health.* SternVitamin GmbH & Co. KG. https://sternvitamin.de/en/mentalhealth/

Substance-Induced Anxiety Disorder. (n.d.). Tufts Medical Center Community Care. Retrieved August 9, 2022, from https://hhma.org/healthadvisor/aha-saanxiet-bha/#:~:text=Substance%2Dinduced%20anxiety%20disorder%20is

Terry, N., & Margolis, K. G. (2017). Serotonergic Mechanisms Regulating the GI Tract: Experimental Evidence and Therapeutic Relevance. *Handbook of Experimental Pharmacology, 239*, 319–342. https://doi.org/10.1007/164_2016_103

Thomson, C. D., Chisholm, A., McLachlan, S. K., & Campbell, J. M. (2008). Brazil nuts: an effective way to improve selenium status. *The American Journal of Clinical Nutrition, 87*(2), 379–384. https://doi.org/10.1093/ajcn/87.2.379

Thyroid disease: How does it affect your mood? (n.d.). Mayo Clinic. https://www.mayoclinic.org/diseases-conditions/hyperthyroidism/expert-answers/thyroid-disease/faq-20058228

Villafuerte, S., & Burmeister, M. (2003). Untangling Genetic Networks of panic, phobia, Fear and Anxiety. *Genome Biology, 4*(8), 224. https://doi.org/10.1186/gb-2003-4-8-224

Water Science School. (2019, May 22). *The Water in You: Water and the Human Body | U.S. Geological Survey.* Www.usgs.gov. https://www.usgs.gov/special-topics/water-science-school/science/water-you-water-and-human-body

Wellness, E. C. +. (2019, August 10). *What Are The Most Common Anxiety Triggers?* Elevate Counseling + Wellness. https://www.elevatecounseling.com/blog-post/what-are-the-most-common-anxiety-triggers

Williams, J. L., Everett, J. M., D'Cunha, N. M., Sergi, D., Georgousopoulou, E. N., Keegan, R. J., McKune, A. J., Mellor, D. D., Anstice, N., & Naumovski, N. (2019). The Effects of Green Tea Amino Acid L-Theanine Consumption on the Ability to Manage Stress and Anxiety Levels: a Systematic Review. *Plant Foods for Human Nutrition.* https://doi.org/10.1007/s11130-019-00771-5

Winters Fisher, A. F. (2019). Dance/movement therapy & warrior wellness: A pilot case study. *The Arts in Psychotherapy, 62,* 52–60. https://doi.org/10.1016/j.aip.2018.11.010

Yang, T., Lai, I. K. W., Bin Fan, Z., & Mo, Q. M. (2021). The impact of a 360° virtual tour on the reduction of psychological stress caused by COVID-19. *Technology in Society, 64*(PMID: 33424061), 101514. https://doi.org/10.1016/j.techsoc.2020.101514

Zamani, M., Alizadeh-Tabari, S., & Zamani, V. (2019). Systematic review with meta-analysis: the prevalence of anxiety and depression in patients with irritable bowel syndrome. *Alimentary Pharmacology & Therapeutics, 50*(2), 132–143. https://doi.org/10.1111/apt.15325